South of the Crisis

South of the Crisis

A Latin American Perspective on the Late Capitalist World

Juan E. Corradi

ANTHEM PRESS
LONDON · NEW YORK · DELHI

Anthem Press
An imprint of Wimbledon Publishing Company
www.anthempress.com

This edition first published in UK and USA 2012
by ANTHEM PRESS
75-76 Blackfriars Road, London SE1 8HA, UK
or PO Box 9779, London SW19 7ZG, UK
and
244 Madison Ave. #116, New York, NY 10016, USA

First published in hardback by Anthem Press in 2010

British Library Cataloguing in Publication Data
A catalogue record for this book is available from the British Library.

Library of Congress Cataloging in Publication Data
A catalog record for this book has been requested.

ISBN-13: 978 0 85728 568 3 (Pbk)
ISBN-10: 0 85728 568 8 (Pbk)

This title is also available as an eBook.

To C. M. S. with love

CONTENTS

LIST OF ILLUSTRATIONS

PREFACE

This book is not a conventional study of Latin America—either in survey fashion or in depth. It is rather a set of polemical perspectives on the dynamics of globalization by a Latin American who stands in a New York observatory. The book contains observations from this center of the global economic crisis, where it originated and then spread like wildfire to the rest of the world, prompting a series of questions about what has happened and what might happen in the countries of the South, in this tempestuous context.

From the bottom of the global South, in Latin America, a small group of *pensadores* gathered in an NGO—The South North Development Initiative— has been voicing their opinions and concerns in the Internet newsletter *Opinión Sur*. As a participant in the group it is my belief that the crisis is an interesting moment of provocation to find a lodestar to sustainable development, a strategy for economic growth with social inclusion. This book is a contribution to that conversation: how the world affects Latin America and how a Latin American perspective can contribute to thinking about the world.

Because the circumstances of my life have caused me to straddle the North and the South, I look at the shifts in global power through different lenses than those whose views reflect the more settled habits of their particular geographies. The vistas that I offer might be of use to readers who wish to look beyond the standard analyses produced within specialized disciplines. In the observations of this book, I have moved away—but not too far—from the field of sociology, which is my academic home, and have used tools from history, politics, and economics. The resulting synthesis, if I were to give it a name, would be one of geopolitics. The label is a bit outmoded, but I like it because it points to an interstitial type of inquiry, one that is free from the fads and foibles of established turfs.

In any discussion of Latin America, the United States is the elephant in the room (some would say that it is the skeleton in the closet). Because of that, the first chapters of the book explore the facets of the crisis in America. There are three reasons for this treatment. First, the crisis has been, initially and foremost, an American crisis. Second, the crisis has revealed and reinforced the limits of

American power. Third, the cracks and fractures in the configuration of world power afford several Latin American countries greater room to establish new alliances and to experiment with novel modes of development.

In fact, this shifting geopolitical context informed my choice of the four countries that appear in the penultimate chapter. I discuss Cuba because for fifty years it resisted American impositions—equipped as it was with a historically obsolete socio-political system. I look at Argentina because the country turned its development away from the international economy that the US had built after the Second World War. Although the Argentine model that Perón set up has not worked well, it has not been superseded in any satisfactory manner; and the nation has declined. Alternatively, Brazil—the only continent-sized country in the region—is poised to become a power in its own right. During most of its history it remained aloof from America and performed fairly well but functioned below its own potential. I include Mexico because that large and fascinating country is the last frontier of the Monroe doctrine. The doctrine has ebbed considerably, but in its retreat it holds on to Mexico with a firm grip. The results have not been encouraging. Mexico faces the difficult task of reforming its own institutions to get better terms in a Faustian deal.

With these considerations in mind, I ask: What is the nature of this crisis? What might be the shape of the world after the crisis runs its course? How will Latin America position itself, as a whole and in its parts, in the post-crisis world? What are the options for the countries in the region? Which paths of development are promising and which ones are blocked? Above all, what ideas should guide Latin Americans in thinking about sustainable development?

My answers to the first bundle of questions are developed throughout the text. They constitute the bulk of it. The last two questions will require extensive treatment in another tome. In various passages of the book and in its last chapter however, I anticipate my general ideas. My response is that, at this point in history, capitalism is the only viable economic system, but it is a system that must be organized and must be tamed. It cannot do that by itself.[1] Left to its own devices, late capitalism derails and damages both the human and the natural environment—what philosophers call the lifeworld.

In order to avoid crises of the present—or even greater—magnitude, every country on the planet, from the most developed to the poorest, will need to launch a program of social inclusion. In a world of astounding accomplishments—whether in science, art, or sport—there are hundreds of millions who are hungry, who are persecuted, or simply left behind. In such an uneven world, the destitute should be assisted without ifs or buts. But those on the rung above them—the other hundreds of millions who are enterprising but frustrated, who do not get far in their endeavors—must first be *equipped* with easier credit, educational opportunities, access not only to cutting–edge technologies but also to state-of-the-art business know-how, and access to world markets. This equipment requires a combination of public, private, and third-sector interventions. The aim should be to help this segment of the people to spark the mobilization of the poor. Perhaps that is the next social revolution, different from those past. In the kitchen of inclusive growth only market forces can take the lead, but what-used-to-be-called socialism should make a good sous-chef.

In economic terms, a strategy of inclusive development operates on three levels, what economists call macro-, meso-, and micro-levels—each one requiring a different mix of agents. At the macro-level the role of the state is indispensable. Nobody else is capable of organizing the market in a comprehensive way and breaking bottlenecks. At the meso-level the agents of development are the large business enterprises, especially those for which "social responsibility" is not just a donation to a good cause or a placating gesture of public relations, but a search down the productive chain for the most impoverished suppliers to help them better themselves and produce in an environmentally friendly way. The micro-level is the area of operation of small communities, local governments, and non-governmental organizations. From micro lending, to small regional banks, to networks of angel investors and venture capital funds, there is today a seething energy at the bottom of the social pyramid in every Latin American country that I know.

In sociological terms, inclusive development means associational participation, beginning in regions and localities. It is this participation, from the bottom up, that can re-energize democracy, and give it content. Associational participation fosters equality in a manner that avoids the pitfalls of state socialism, which follows an inverse sequence—from the top down, leading to economic dysfunctions, political repression, and demoralization.

In political terms, the challenge of inclusive development is how to arrive at a durable consensus without authoritarian imposition, on the one hand, or gridlock, on the other. It means nothing less than reinventing democracy in what some analysts have called a post-democratic age.[2]

These considerations take place against a backdrop of sweeping geopolitical changes. I had the luck of bearing witness to some of these changes. In 1999 I was the executive director of Villa La Pietra, a grand estate in Florence, bequeathed by Sir Harold Acton to New York University. The university organized at La Pietra a meeting of world leaders under the cheery rubric "progressive governance for the twenty first century." The theme was broad and fairly vague. The gathering was, in reality, an occasion to celebrate two things: the joint Western "humanitarian intervention" in carving Yugoslavia, and the fact that the participating leaders came from the left but had transcended their own provenance to organize responsibly the world. Somebody remarked that it was like a meeting of driving instructors: you enter the vehicle from the left, and you drive it on the right. Seven of them came: the President of the United States, the German Chancellor, the British Prime Minister, the French Premier, the President of the Italian Council of Ministers, the Prime Minister of Portugal, and the President of Brazil. The university acted as a host and as a broker. As a university officer in residence, I had to help with the logistics and organize the dinner for two hundred guests. It took five months of preparations to get everybody and everything in place. During the preparatory period I was the proverbial fly on the wall, privy to conversations that were off-the-cuff and off the record. I shall not disclose them but I can share two of my observations. First, it took considerable effort for the Europeans to convince the delegation from the United States to include Brazil. "Why should we?" and "Who are they to share the table?" were questions asked more than once. In the end, given the prestige of President Fernando Henrique Cardoso, the Americans relented. Second, the sizes of the delegations revealed more than just the number of bodies. All chief executives save one arrived with retinues that ranged from five to fifty. The US President traveled with seven hundred. In Florence, America was acting like the new Rome.

A month later I was in Beijing, welcoming Y2K with friends in the Great Hall of the People; fireworks over Tiananmen Square accompanied our celebration. What I saw at the time astonished me, especially the breakneck pace of Chinese growth. Since then I have returned to China, between trips to South America, only to find the pace even more intense than before. A decade has passed since the summit in Florence. How the world has changed since then! In 2010 the United States seems to have lowered its ambitions. China is the second world power and Brazil has become a global player that everybody is now eager to invite.

ACKNOWLEDGEMENTS

This book would not have been possible without the support of enabling environments, personal and institutional. I wish to thank the team of *Opinión Sur* in Buenos Aires for supplying a forum where to publish and test my ideas. Several chapters first took shape as reflections shared in those pages. In New York, the board of the South North Development Initiative, of which I was president, was always a good sounding board. The Department of Sociology at New York University has been benign enough to make me arrive at my office every day sporting a smile.

My annual pilgrimage to Lucca to give a month-long seminar at the Institute of Advanced Studies (IMT) afforded me the luxury of reflection and the opportunity of discussion with young scholars from all over the world. I owe a special debt of gratitude to my late friend Victor Zaslavsky for good advice and extraordinary insights on the transitions from non-democratic to democratic systems, and from state-socialist societies to free-market ones. We taught several seminars together to great success. Our doctoral students produced excellent research and taught us much in return. In Rome, the General Secretary of the Italian-Latin American Institute (IILA), Ambassador Paolo Bruni, was kind enough to invite me to present my ideas in the beautiful *palazzo* where things Latin American are displayed and discussed. But Paolo opened other doors before: to the fascinating world of resurgent China, when he was ambassador in Beijing. To him go many thanks.

On Latin America in general and Brazil in particular, I have had the privilege of life-long conversations with Hélio Jaguaribe and Anna Maria Jaguaribe, father and daughter, whose luminous visions of possibility opened my mind. On Argentina, I received an array of help from long-time friends, but I have learned the most from my many conversations with Juan Carlos Torre. On Mexico, I have followed from the distant proximity of the Internet the opinions and positions of my old friend John Saxe Fernandez of the UNAM. On Cuba, Nicaragua, Costa Rica, Colombia, Chile and the other nations of the Western hemisphere, I met many experts, perused statistics, and observed what I observed, but I was mostly in the silent company of documents and books. Juan Rial has kept me abreast of the politics of the moment in various countries of Latin America, from Uruguay to Honduras.

On the broader world and on global social and economic issues, I am self-taught. An insatiable voyager by air, land, and sea (in my own sailboat I've crossed oceans), I have received many gifts of hospitality in near and far places, from the tropics to the Arctic. A wave of special thanks goes to friends in Norway, Sweden, Denmark, and Finland for showing me (quite unbeknownst to them) that social institutions, which in other latitudes are deemed incompatible, can, in fact, be happily combined—provided the will is there, and the public cultivated, serious, and decent.

I owe special thanks to Moira Hodgson for putting me in touch, through the good offices of Nan Talese, with Lorna Owen, who copy edited the text with professional diligence and good cheer.

All these gracious people helped me write this book. Its mistakes are solely mine.

I have been a lucky man: the goodwill with which I have been graced has been enhanced, multiplied and topped by the company and steadfast support, as well as editorial help, of Christina Spellman, to whom I am married. Lest I forget, for several months my writing retreats were kindly shared by Churchill, a devoted canine friend. If only dogs could vote.

INTRODUCTION

A Provocation

Before the global financial crisis exploded, social change on the planet seemed as vigorous as it was problematic: awesome technological development; the emergence of new vibrant economies such as China, India, and Brazil; marked inequality between countries and within them; persistent poverty in most parts of the world; continued destruction of the environment; deviation of resources toward financial speculation; growth of economic bubbles and occasional blowouts, terrorism and violence, genocide and civil war, epidemics. These were a few of the challenges that faced humanity in the new millennium—conflicts and conundrums stemming from the deep-rooted way in which so many of the countries had been functioning. Then the crisis arrived at the very center of the global system. Panic ensued, and political authorities in most nations hastily adopted emergency measures.

Today different ways out of the global crisis are being tried. Some of the solutions have led me to think that we are rebuilding the pre-crisis world instead of transforming it, while other efforts seem focused on rethinking who we are and what we aspire to become so that we may choose a better global direction. The struggle that marks the beginning of the second decade of the twenty-first century will determine whether a collective course and way of functioning will be adjusted for everyone's good or just for the good of a few.

Transitions

The geopolitical balance of the first decade of the twenty-first century reveals several major shifts. On the security front, global war has faded into the past. It has been replaced by nuclear proliferation, a greater risk of more regional wars, and one major new challenge: international terrorism. On the economic front, capitalism has encountered its own limits. Major crises have moved from the periphery to the center. The South, on the other hand, has shown signs of development and growth, aided and abetted by the multi-polarization of power. Latin America, in particular, can no longer be considered a unitary zone. Diversity is increasing, in part fuelled by the ebb of American power.

Ten years after the millennium, the world is in the midst of a bewildering transition—from West to East, from an anarchic capitalism to a regulated one, from a type of development indifferent to the environment to one that is more mindful of it, from wars between states to a pattern of collective (in)security, from closed ideologies to open-ended and pragmatic codes. These patterns are not all bad. The risks, however, are many, and some of them are enormous.

We have left behind the great tragedies of the twentieth century but also many of its hopes and illusions. Socialism was unable to top capitalism and failed as an alternative in the countries where it was installed. Capitalism, in turn, has been unable to overcome major contradictions. Democracy has spread around the world but it has lost its advantage and now faces a crisis of commitment and representation. Progress has been noted on many counts: human longevity, the gathering, retrieval, and transmission of information, technical prowess, knowledge of the brain; but progress is uneven, and its unintended consequences have placed the environment and the quality of life of future generations at risk. Humanity is crowded, and the earth is tired.

War and Peace

In the past crises have often resulted in wars, and war has been billed as a remedy to crisis. In these times war is asymmetrical and transversal. The acquisition of nuclear weapons by newcomer states makes them weigh the logic of deterrence, which during the cold war was a guarantor of peace—albeit an armed peace. We have now moved from a bipolar to a multipolar deterrence. The risk of an accidental nuclear war has therefore increased in direct proportion to proliferation. But even in this case, the higher probability is of a local, not general, nuclear exchange.

There is another challenge, however. Nuclear weapons may fall into the hands of non-state actors, such as terrorist networks. The detonation of one or more such devices in the very heart of the "civilized," highly "protected" world is a probable occurrence, precisely because the world is more interconnected than ever before. In other words, anything may happen anywhere.

The millennium started with the spectacular attack of 9/11, which was followed by similar attacks in various cities of the West and of the East. To date there has been no satisfactory response to these challenges and no effective—preventive or retaliatory—solution has been found. In asymmetrical warfare, the attackers use low-cost resources and can tolerate failure upon failure because a single successful hit can make up for the unsuccessful ones. In contrast, the defenders are compelled to use immense resources with very poor results. Only 100 per cent "success" could be considered "victory." There is no strategic theory and/or doctrine capable of a comprehensive response to bellicose asymmetry. The high military commands of the world as well as a great number of think tanks have libraries full of papers and books on the subject, but the vast majority have one problem: they were written by losers.[1]

The decade closes with uncertainty and ambiguity, exemplified in President Obama's speech that he delivered in 2009 on the occasion of receiving the Nobel Peace Prize. The address was not a discourse on peace but one on international security in the face of nihilistic, asymmetrical attacks. Just as two thousand years ago peace meant *pax romana*, so today peace is seen in the West as *pax americana*. We should, however, remember what the historian Tacitus said with regard to the earlier attempt: *ubi solitudinem faciunt pacem appellant*, or "Where they create desolation they call it peace."

East and West

When the former Chinese prime minister Zhou Enlai (the faithful and aristocratic companion of Mao) was asked what he thought of the French Revolution, he famously answered, "It is too early to tell." And the Indian spiritual and political leader Mahatma Gandhi, when asked what he thought of Western civilization, responded, "I think it would be a good idea." The vision of the world espoused by these great Asian leaders is very different from the visions of the West. Despite the stunning pace of change in the East and South Asia, the inhabitants of these lands have a distinct sense of time and an ironic perspective on the impatience of the West.[2] To them geopolitical oscillations are no surprise. Once their nations were at the very center of the civilized world. Later they lost ground to Europe and the United States, and now they are reclaiming much of that lost ground. The West has taken a step back, the East and the South two steps forward.

A special feature of the present oscillation is the speed and ease with which the peoples of Asia can absorb, adapt, and develop Western science and technology—without giving up their patterns of behavior. Different from many postcolonial peoples on other continents, Asians do not seem to suffer a crisis of identity. Once, while I was in China, a high official of the government told a Western diplomat friend of mine that his country's leadership consisted of pragmatic engineers responsible for the care and feeding of 1.3 billion people in a globalized world; they were at once fully aware of the challenge and completely convinced that "China is eternal." His remarks suggested a unique combination of tradition and modernity, technocracy and forbearance, of speedy adaptation and the long view. In India the formula is a different one (it is after all the largest English-speaking democracy in the world), but it combines just as much the old with the new. Here is the paradox: in our globalized world the emerging powers are not young nations but ancient ones. Older "new nations" (for example, Argentina and the United States) seem somewhat out of place; they are too set in their ways to innovate, on the one hand, and too young to be wise on the other.

A Verdict on Globalization

At this point in time the geopolitical balance is ambiguous. One more decade has passed in which the process of globalization has continued, and the world seems like a body with overdeveloped limbs but a weak heart. From an economic standpoint, most of the periphery is poised to continue a sustained growth, albeit not as spectacular as it once was. Such growth will not depend as much as before on the Western locomotive. It will depend more on internal demand and on the incorporation of billions of the world's poorest people to lower-middle class consumption.

Advanced capitalism is likely to suffer from idle capacity and high unemployment. There will be a continued need for state intervention and for more regulation of the economy. The West seems bound for a curious fate: the initiator of globalism has become its victim. Perched as I am in the United States, it seems to me that—contrary to other forms of capitalism, such as those in Scandinavia, that are steadier and more equitable but marginal—American capitalism has been a casualty of its own success in the post-Cold War era. The existence of a serious rival had kept it disciplined.[3] The disappearance of such an enemy, and the consequent opening of the former communist world, enabled American capitalism to grow without oversight; the US displaced its productive base abroad and became over-financed. In the end, its economy stalled.

On the way to this sorry outcome, American capitalism managed to turn its illusions into a hegemonic ideological school. The first decade of the century saw the spread of a neoliberal creed around the world. The doctrine sponsored policies that disassembled hitherto structured countries East and South. Many of the reforms were inappropriate and incomplete, and left a number of nations, notably in Latin America, struggling to put their disparate fragments together again. A series of financial crises in those countries at the beginning of the decade of 2000 foreshadowed, though unbeknownst to most, a larger crisis at the center by the decade's end.

The Americas, North and South

In Latin America progress in the first ten years of this century has been mixed although better than in "the lost decade" at the end of the twentieth century.[4] In general terms, growth has occurred but not a truly sustainable development. Social inequality remains intolerably high, social disarticulation has become worse both inside the countries of the region and between them, and dependency has not come to an end—it changed partners and patterns instead. The perspectives for the region can best be described in Jorge Luis Borges's words as a "garden of forking paths,"[5] or in Max Weber's image of history, as a railway network with several switch points.[6]

The panorama prompts me to ask some questions: What will be the future of Cuba, which is today a living museum of the defunct Soviet-type societies? How do we explain the resilience of Argentina—which grows economically through its food and other exports and yet declines socially and politically, resembling ever more other Latin American countries that Argentines once arrogantly despised? How can we evaluate the advancement of Brazil as a world power, though not a regional one, and the emergence there of a massive new middle class? Where is this giant going, and why is it behaving—in the words of Andrés Malamud, like "a leader without followers"?[7] How to encompass in a single gaze the smaller countries that are as different from each other as the larger ones: peaceful and mature Uruguay, politically and ecologically correct Costa Rica, and banana-republican Honduras? Whither Venezuela, where an oil-corrupted party democracy has been replaced by a personalized redistributive and plebiscitary one? What to make of Chile who seems to belong to the Asia-Pacific area more than to its own neighborhood? Can Mexico backtrack from the often choking embrace of NAFTA (the North American Free Trade Association)?[8] What will be the long-term upshot of the Andean indigenous majorities' political mobilization—a process that both integrates and polarizes at the same time? What is the verdict on Latin American democracies that seem to have passed the test of time but still face, here and there, threats of coups and "democratic destitution" of their governments? The panorama is much too varied to justify a single overview.

There is, however, a common geopolitical denominator to this bewildering diversity: the vacuum of power left by the United States's decline as the indispensable single influence and point of reference. A voice from the North seems to whisper, "We are otherwise engaged, and you are on your own, my friends." From the South, in turn, another voice softly answers, "We are no longer the Other. Look at our failures and our crises and think for a moment in the old Latin adage: *de te fabula narratur* (of you the tale is told)."[9] The tables were not turned, but this is a different world from that of only ten years ago.

The Problems Ahead

With the addition of 3 billion people to the markets of the planet, the growth of the global economy has brought benefits such as a reduction of poverty and access to middle-class status for more than 200 million people. But several factors now threaten such achievements: limited energy supplies,[10] food shortage and high prices, climate change, and a social inequality that is huge and visible. Add to these crises of scarcity the cyclical crises of excess: an unmanageable surplus of goods largely due to the concentration of earnings. Solutions to these problems can be imagined but will not necessarily be implemented. A rational society may be what we all need; it seems to be, however, a type of society that nobody wants. The spontaneous dynamics of a capitalist economy and the crosscurrents of politics block it.

In the opinion of knowledgeable economists Latin America has been spared the worst of the crisis.[11] The various countries of the region have responded differently, and their respective prospects for the future also vary. But the main difference between them has more to do with the nature of prior reforms and with internal politics than with the impact of outside forces. In other words "path dependency"[12] is strong. However, the cracks and fissures that have grown in the global capitalist world, and the geopolitical shifts that accompany them, have opened new opportunities to those who are well poised to take advantage of them.

In this shifting world two immense countries must be watched: Brazil, in the West and China, in the East. Brazil has the potential to become both a regional power (although it has yet to do this well) and a world player, as a member of the BRICs (the acronym for Brazil, Russia, India, China that Goldman Sachs first used in a thesis projecting the economic potential of those countries). For other Latin American countries that wish to free themselves from the exclusive tutelage of the United States, China and Brazil offer, if not assurance, at least a measure of insurance. Beyond the actuarial benefit, these two mega countries may also propose a model of development that combines economic growth with social inclusion. Yet, even in the most optimistic scenarios, if social progress is achieved only as a byproduct of thoughtless and breakneck growth, the world of the future may face crises of a magnitude that could make the current one seem like a vicar's tea party.

The Bane of Concentration

In principle it is easy to imagine a society that is unequal but not impoverished. That is the promise of prosperity. It is the very basis for the legitimacy of the capitalist system. It is also a mirage. The lure of profit has led many to believe that poverty can be "solved" by the trickling down of wealth from ever-greater heights. They do not perceive that a high concentration of wealth has serious social dysfunctions and that it produces, in the end, a crash. Social inequality stands behind many calamities in both the developed and developing world, in rich countries as well as in poor countries. Adolescent pregnancies, early deaths, homicide, mental illnesses, bad student formation, packed prisons, and drugs (whether refined cocaine for the suburbs or crack for the shanty towns) are social problems that can be traced to persistent inequality.[13] These social problems fester in societies where there is a big gap between the classes. In order to minimize these ills, jails are built, doctors become specialized, social workers, education specialists and an army of sociologists intervene, rehabilitation clinics are set up, and large sums of money are allotted to ministries of welfare. Those services manage the dysfunctions and sustain a sizeable portion of the middle class, but do not address the causes of poverty. It would be cheaper and more satisfactory to attack those root causes using good structural public policies, aimed at reducing the economic and social distance existing between the rich and the poor.

There are obviously many alternative ways of lessening inequality according to the cultural and ideological peculiarity of each society. In Sweden, for instance, inequality is reduced through the tax system, while in Japan this is achieved by reducing salary differences—both are a direct intervention in the income distribution system. The US does not use either of these two strategies, but sometimes inequality is mitigated through employees' participation programs that allow partial ownership of the companies they work for. The American formula, though still burdened by the legacy of racism, has favored "starting point" opportunities in a competitive social system. As in sports, the game is legitimized by notions of fair play and by a wide distribution of opportunities. In Latin America, there have been repeated attempts at income redistribution through patronage, subsidies, and the national takeover of productive assets—all with generally negative results. The roads are different, the aims are similar, but a harsh truth remains: inequality within, between, and across societies is on the rise.[14]

In the United States in recent decades there has been an extraordinary concentration of income. Today the economic disparity in the country is greater than that of any other developed nations. In the developing world, the huge rates of growth in emerging markets have also increased inequality both internally and externally. In China, home to the "miracle" growth, the income gap between the coastal and inland areas is as big as between the United States and North Africa.

In broad strokes, such concentration of wealth results in two effects. First, rising inequality introduces a toxic dynamic that influences society as a whole. Health and longevity are negatively affected. There is less social mobility and more resentment. The poor in these rich but very unequal societies feel more deprived than do the poor in less wealthy but more egalitarian societies. The dynamic is not new. Reflecting on the causes of the French Revolution, Alexis de Tocqueville reached the following conclusion: it was not poverty that triggered the revolt, but the injustices perceived in uneven progress. Perhaps there is a lesson here for the creation of public policies in countries of the North as well as in those of the South: strategies that reduce inequality produce a better quality of life and reduce social tensions. The second effect of rising inequality is systemic. The real economy is travestied in a show of smoke and mirrors. A high concentration of wealth fosters financial speculation at one end (the unproductive use of excess funds) and indebtedness at the other (mass consumption with insufficient funds). These related processes have led the principal economy of the global system into its worst crisis since the Great Depression.

Precarious Progress

In the last twenty years many millions of people have come out of poverty and have achieved a modest position amid the middle social strata. Yet, how safe is their position? To answer this question it is useful to refer to the Middle Class Safety Index, created by the Heller School for Social Policy and Management of Brandeis University, Massachusetts.[15] This index combines 5 economic variables, as follows: capital goods a family owns, level of education, housing cost, family shopping basket budget, and medical expenses. According to the combined range of those variables, a family or a group of families—that is a social sector—can be classified as "safe," "marginal," or "at risk." In the US, reputedly the wealthiest country of all, Brandeis researchers applied the Index to the ethnic groups that have most recently achieved a middle class status: African-American, Hispanics, Latinos. Results show how precarious their situation is. According to the research team director, Professor Thomas Shapiro, financial health eludes most of the African-American and Latino middle classes. The great progress they have made at school, at work, and income-wise, are being eroded by the lack of capitalization (or indebtedness level) that undermines the financial security of these two groups of middle class families. According to this study, there are two primary destabilizing causes: the lack of savings and the housing costs. Only 2 per cent of African-American families and 8 per cent of Hispanic families have savings that allow them to survive nine months should they lose their main source of income. We can conclude that in the US these groups who have recently entered the middle class are at risk. Only a wrinkle in any of the above-mentioned items—a mortgage crisis, a serious illness, the loss of a source of income would suffice for a middle class family to drop in status. As an antidote to this precariousness, experts recommend educational re-training at a lower cost than current tuition charges, a higher level of savings, the reduction of personal debt, and universal and cheaper health insurance.

If the newest mid-strata in a "mature" developed society such as the US can find themselves in an unstable economic situation, could this also happen—although for different reasons—to the hundreds of millions of people in the great emerging countries who have gained lower middle class status as a consequence of the recent Asian economic drive? We do not have a "security index" for these countries' middle classes—it is pressing, however, to generate one similar to the one used by the Brandeis team yet modifying the variables.[16] In such an index both the financial juggling and the private indebtedness that affect the American middle class would have much less bearing while the family shopping basket—in particular food—would be much more important. But their achievements are very fragile too.

The case of food in the globalized economy illustrates the tenuousness of social achievements. In emerging markets (India and China for example) the precariousness found in the rising strata stems from the clash of opposite forces. On the one hand, the new middle strata emulate the consumption of their counterparts in developed countries. Their demand exerts great pressure on food prices. But the industrial development to which they owe their progress requires fuel and raw materials, which in turn, leads to higher prices of inputs and higher costs of food.[17] In addition the world-wide scramble for sources of energy leads to a reduction of the agricultural production of food in favor of growing bio-fuels. The result is a considerable and continuous rise in food prices that threatens, in some cases, the survival of the poorest as well as the status of the newly minted middle class. Governments are tempted to adopt protectionist measures that restrict trade and end up being counterproductive. A vicious circle is thus generated within the process of global economic development itself. We could face a planetary crisis of neo-Malthusian nature. A Malthusian crisis is a return to the conditions in the subsistence sphere that English mathematician Thomas Malthus (1766-1834) predicted as a result of a population growth that exceeds agricultural production. The present day discussion on development sustainability indicates that we have not come out of the Malthusian trap, except it has a "global" twist. In China, according to some estimates, the livelihood of 100 million agricultural workers is threatened as World Trade Organization rules increase China's dependence on foreign food supplies. A prospect that could be good for a country like Argentina could frighten the rulers in Beijing. For the moment, they have decided to fall forward rather than scale back. That is the logic of global markets, but does it suffice?

Obstacles to Reason

A solution to the problems mentioned above would begin with a coordination of public policies on the part of all the governments, as the system is interdependent and global. But that coordination—owing to the absence of a worldwide government—is the most difficult tool to forge, since the sovereignty of states, though diminished, is still strong enough to block any serious attempt toward a joint sacrifice or international solidarity.

Global leadership is nowadays in the hands of about 6,000 people—that is to say, one person for each million inhabitants on Earth—of whom around half are multibillionaires. The group gets together periodically for symposiums such as the World Economic Forum in Davos, Switzerland. The ensemble can be described as a global power elite, a super class—or using an old Soviet term, a *Nomenklatura*: a list of permanent and temporary leaders—of their "sherpas" and dolphins. For the moment no coordinated solution for the major planetary problems has emerged from any of their meetings.

Yet, there is a possibility that with the adoption of difficult yet rational policies among leaders with the greatest capacity for action some solutions may be found. We are witnessing the end of an era in which energy and food were cheap goods. From now on they will be more expensive and scarce.[18] In a few years we will experience the global shortage of another good that was until now public and free: water. I strongly fear that the true motivation to resolve any of these issues will come with the seriousness of the crisis itself, and with one or another catalyzing catastrophe. Crisis has become a substitute for planning.

Whither Latin America?

As the hard times stretch out, the countries of the Latin South are in fairly good shape to face them as long as their governments do not get distracted with adventures or carried away by the so-called exports "tail wind." The economies of the Latin American region, with the important exception of Mexico, have shown surprising resilience during the Great Recession—now referred to as the Third Depression,[19] which is one of the worst economic downturns in modern history. Most of the countries in the region avoided the borrowing spree that traditionally followed previous crises in the developing and in the developed world. How long they will continue on this virtuous path remains an open-ended question, especially in those countries—Venezuela and Argentina for example—in which populist governments will face increasing difficulties in combining fiscal discipline with payoffs to their voters.

With a fragile economic recovery in the first world and fears of a "double-dip recession" and even the prospect of a Japanese-style "lost decade" ahead, how can Latin American countries return to the high growth rates of the recent past in order to sustain development and—in the best of cases like Brazil—support a rising middle class? Whether populist or not, Latin American countries could fall into a vulnerable financial condition if they do not grow at a fast clip. If recovery in the first world cannot help, the question then is: will the Asian countries provide the locomotive for the required growth? Common economic wisdom states that growth rates above 6 per cent are necessary to improve living standards in most of these countries. Unlike those in the first world, Latin American countries are not "over the hump" in development, so they are unable to function well at low levels of growth. The challenge of inclusion—bringing the poor and the destitute into the system (in many cases "back in")—demands high levels of activity, and a new radical imagination. The radical blueprints of the past have proven either illusory or nightmarish.

So far, Latin America did quite well in this crisis, better in fact than most observers expected. For those with a longer historical memory, its performance recalls a similar experience in the 1930s,[20] when many countries in the region also managed to weather the storm. At that time Latin Americans came out of the crisis with fairly original theories of development, and fairly unorthodox patterns of growth.[21] Based on the strategy of import-substituting industrialization (ISI) (the push for producing locally industrialized goods), the modality worked for a few decades but eventually it led to a series of national crises. It became clear that the Latin American way was of out of sync with the modalities of growth in the rest of the world. A new orientation and a new mix of policies are now required—in short a new type of heterodoxy.

Globalization today has produced an international division of labor that bears a partial resemblance to that of a hundred years ago. As China's industrialization follows the course of other developed nations, its demand for infrastructure will peak long before food consumption, especially a higher quality of food consumption.[22] This creates opportunities for several Latin American countries, long specialized in the export of foodstuffs. China today consumes more protein but has far to go to catch up with the developed world. Per capita consumption of meat is less than 100 pounds. The cattle breeders of the Southern Cone should rejoice—provided governments do not constrain them in order to flatter the stomachs of their electoral base.[23] In turn, raising more animals requires feed, and growing this grain increases the demand for fertilizer. In general, Latin agribusiness is on a roll with the largest spurt of world demand since the 1900s.

Today, as in the past, in order to do well Latin American countries need strong, predictable, and sustainable growth. They have to seize the opportunities afforded by comparative advantage, but also diversify the economies and find within them new industrial and service niches.[24] Now as well as then, theory and practice must move away from established orthodoxies—notably neoliberal doctrines—and be in sync with the dynamics of emerging powers.[25] But just as the developed world has failed to produce a new John Maynard Keynes, so Latin America has not produced a new Raúl Prebisch. Meanwhile, in the North and in the South, mired in mediocrity, we wait.[26]

Chapter One

IMPENDING STORMS: FISCAL INTEMPERANCE AND MORAL DILEMMAS

At the beginning of the new century the volatility of the dollar betrayed the structural weakness of the American economy, an economy based on indebted consumption and enormous military spending. In my native Argentina I spoke to many citizens through whose eyes I could see the first signs of a potential geopolitical restructuring and the incipient emergence of new blocs. Those Argentines were always interested in the broader world as well as in my experiences on the ocean as an offshore sailor.

It wasn't easy explaining to them how tropical cyclones take shape and grow—the kind of storms called hurricanes when they batter the Atlantic and typhoons when unleashed in the Pacific. However, I tried my best, since I found they served a perfect analogy. A hurricane takes shape gradually at first, but then strikes with catastrophic results. Moist air from warm waters rises to phenomenal heights (from the atmosphere to the troposphere, grazing the stratosphere). The navigator's barometer registers a tremendous drop in atmospheric pressure. The mass of air rises in a revolving fashion. In the Northern Hemisphere, this revolution is counter-clockwise. Upon reaching the highest strata the air mass, instead of running into a reverse air flow that would brake its circulation, runs into another current flowing in the same direction that imparts amazing velocity to this high cloud spiral—speeds in excess of 74 miles per hour. This mass of spinning air moves like a crazy merry-go-round around a small, calm center or eye. The huge whirlwind, with a diameter hundreds of miles wide, moves over the ocean, following the warm water currents it feeds on. It destroys everything in its path: large and small boats, shacks and hotels, villages and plantations, lives and dreams. Only two things can stop it: the large continental masses where hurricanes generally make landfall after sweeping islands and coastlines, or the colder high-latitude waters where they cool down and lose power. The atmosphere recovers its equilibrium when the tremendous energy stored in the tropics is discharged in the planet's temperate zones. The sole thing a sailor can do in these cases is stay home, if possible, for the duration of hurricane season, or ride it out offshore, trusting that prudent measures will outweigh the violence of nature.

At that point, it was easier for me to explain the stormy forces at work in the international monetary markets. When North American consumers buy huge quantities of Asian products[1] (the majority of global production has moved from other countries to China and other Asian sites), hundreds of billions of dollars from these sales accumulate in the coffers of Asian governments who, in turn, recycle this money through the North American financial system and, in this way, influence the interest rates and economic activity of the world's leading superpower. At this point in my explanation, I made a drawing as an illustration (Figure 1) so my listeners could visualize the global economic flow.

I explained that bonds are a type of IOU. If the debtor gets in a jam, and stops paying, the cessation of payment is called default. Default leads to a huge crisis, since monetary flows break down and the trust on which transactions are based is violated. An alternative is to renegotiate the terms of repayment. Another alternative is to pay with devalued currency, which is a more delicate way of paying back less than what you owe (if the country has the privilege of going into debt with its own money, and this money is reserve currency).[2]

Argentines, with surprising speed, were able to boil down my explanation in terms of their own experience. "Look," one of them said, "when a country spends more than it earns, and takes out loans to keep on spending, sooner or later it runs the risk of going broke. It's at the mercy of its foreign creditors who impose their own conditions." She added, "The country then is full of poor, angry people. And they have every right to be angry—if their savings have gone up in smoke and they only have a few worthless pesos in their pockets, and they have unpayable debts on top of that."[3]

Some of my interlocutors had been lucky. Others not. In 2001 the sovereign default of Argentina snuck up on them with devastating force. The luckier ones had their savings in cash dollars in a safe. Others were caught with their savings in formerly convertible pesos that suddenly lost three-fourths of their value. Some avoided being corralled and having their captive dollars forcefully converted into worthless local currency at the unfavorable "official" rate. They felt safer since they could gradually change their green bills into pesos on the black market and, in this way, hold out in the hope of better times. However, they read in the papers that the dollar was also losing its value against other currencies.

I confirmed their diagnosis and added an even harsher prognosis of my own: The dollar would keep losing value, although it was hard to say whether this descent would be gradual or abrupt or just when it would come to an end.[4]

Figure 1: Global Circulation of Money, or the Making of a Financial Hurricane

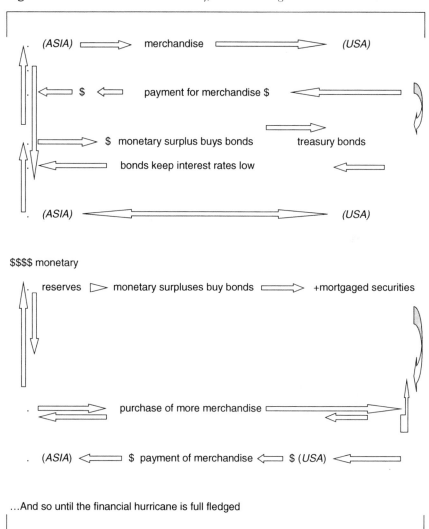

I advised them to move part of their savings from dollars to other currencies and to put that money into European and other securities with a prudent term. But economic forecasting is a lot like weather forecasting: we know that there is a risk of bad weather, but we can't be sure whether the clouds taking shape on the horizon portend a passing storm or a tropical cyclone. I went back to my sailing yarn: It's best to stay in the shelter of a good port, observe the situation, and wait.

That said, I made it clear that this time we weren't dealing with an isolated storm on the periphery but a global imbalance that would affect the entire planet. Through the purchase of securities and bonds, China, Japan, and other Asian countries lend money to the United States in order to ensure the maintenance of a high level of consumption and, in turn, the absorption of the huge productive surplus from Asia. The low interest rates in the United States enable citizens, through commercial, personal, and mortgage credit, to indebt themselves by consuming. Until 2002, the time of my conversations, this imbalanced flow was sustained without too many glitches, with low inflation and cheap money. But, inevitably, two simultaneous phenomena occur at the poles of the system, as Figure 1 indicates. On one side, the Asian economies develop, and a huge productive surplus builds up in the Pacific sector. On the other side of the ocean, public and private indebtedness increase and bubbles of fictitious capital form,[5] for instance, the rise in real estate values, mainly mortgaged properties.

This upward spiral is dangerous, just like the initial phase of a cyclone's growth. The imbalance generates pressure on the dollar that prompts its devaluation. The Asian countries resist revaluing their currencies since that would lead to an increase in the prices of their products, and consequently, a reduction in their exports as well as a significant cut in the value of their securities held in dollars. With good reason, they advise that the United States reduce its fiscal deficit; in other words, that the government of the world's superpower spend less. But taking US international policy into consideration and, in particular, its enormous military spending, that common sense solution becomes problematic. War is costly—even more costly when you don't sacrifice consumption. The great North American geopolitical dilemma can be summed up in a few words: indebted consumption + a war left out of the approved budget and without increased taxes to pay for it = the crisis of the dollar. That is inevitable in the long run.

The geopolitical corollary was clear and not very promising. In the West the great Atlantic alliance that materialized after World War II was breaking up. But this Atlantic disturbance whose first rumblings had been heard, though serious, did not carry with it the potentially devastating force of a typhoon in the Pacific. This other storm could strike if Japan and China decided to convert their reserves to other currencies, and move their investments to other markets. But between now and then, there would be many ups and downs in currencies.

The foregoing speculations took place in 2001, in a peripheral nation undergoing a sovereign default of unprecedented proportions but one that nobody thought at the time could occur in the developed countries of the North.

The Storm

The US economic crisis started with the insolvency of the most modest home mortgage holders in one corner of the economy, then spread very fast throughout the financial sector, causing a further decline of an already weakened dollar and in short order uncertainty in all global markets.

When a minor cause produces major effects, that very disproportion is a symptom that the great underlying structures are weaker than we had believed. In the US there was no more talk of a "soft landing"—it was in a full emergency landing. Economic difficulties affected quite elevated sectors of society. The New York stock market indices declined precipitously. The dollar lost its value day-by-day. The mortgage crisis turned into a collective panic. And on top of all this, according to the opinion of economists Joseph Stiglitz and Winda Bilmes,[6] the disastrous war in Iraq reached an estimated total spending of $3 trillion.

Washington no longer heard the Republican siren song promising domestic prosperity without sacrifice and foreign-policy arrogance without counsel. The various speculative bubbles burst one-by-one in the developed world. In the countries to the South nobody knew if this would also be the fate of the so-called commodities—metals, hydrocarbons, meat, and grain—boom. When the bubbles burst, a more moderate reality could be seen, although its symptoms were concealed by the uninterrupted chitchat of the media.

Behind the glitter of credit consumption stood 37 million people, out of 300 million, in dire poverty (many of them children). If we add the 60 million whose families live on an annual income ranging from $20,000 to $40,000, the picture that emerges is not a flattering one. In the richest country on earth, almost one third of the population lives on the edge. Their jobs are precarious and can easily be lost. They have trouble meeting their financial obligations and paying their bills. The result is a palpable fear—of others, of disasters, of illness, of unemployment, and also of the government. At the bottom of the social pyramid, resentment prepares the ground for demagoguery.[7]

The fear that springs from the bottom of society has reached the middle sectors—those whose annual income ranges from $50,000 to $100,000. They are the proverbial American middle class: the emblem of a way of life, and of a whole civilization. Today they are subject to what I like to call a strong social compression that, in turn, leads to intergenerational descent. The much-touted American dream seems to be at wit's end. Stagnation has produced a profound crisis of identity for America—something both economists and sociologists are bound to investigate for years to come. The structural problems of reduced mobility and greater inequality were partially hidden by the availability of cheap debt—a cushion that the crisis has removed. As a result, anger is growing and is becoming increasingly political. Michael Spence, a Nobel Prize-winning economist who has led a four-year study into the future of global growth, had this to say, "The future I most fear for America is Latin American: a grossly unequal society that is prone to wild swings from populism to orthodoxy, which makes sensible government increasingly hard to imagine."[8]

Fifty years ago middle-class Americans could rely on satisfactory and stable jobs, on prospects of significant salary improvements, and on the hope for an even better future for their children. They could count on a nice house in the suburbs, one or two family cars, a mortgage amortized over 30 years, and a free-from-anguish retirement at the end of the road. In general, only one adult in the family (of an average four-member family) would work. Nowadays those jobs that make such lifestyle possible have become scarce.

To cope with the shortage of good secure jobs, the middle class was forced to use other strategies. In the average family, instead of only one adult being employed, now there are two working members. Wives and mothers went back to work. The cloud had a silver lining: this need for another income was seen as an advance in gender equality, by freeing women from their traditional family roles. Yet, the harsh economic reality was that now to keep the same standard of living two jobs were needed where before one was enough. Men and women also started to work longer hours and to have shorter holidays. In some cases they had to handle several jobs at a time. They all had to march faster in order to remain in place. The image that comes to mind is that of a whole social class on a treadmill. Economists, however, hailed those changes once they verified an increase in productivity.

Finally, individuals and families resorted to personal and mortgage credit to keep the standard of living they were used to. Rather than saving they ran further into debt. The American dream was being bought on multiple installments. All these factors together make up the social compression of the middle class. This compression leads them to fear that their children will not enjoy a more comfortable life or a better future, otherwise referred to as intergenerational descent. It signals pessimism in a social class that was traditionally devoted to the idea of progress in every domain.

Furthermore, in the portion of society we may call the leading sector, the power elite or the dominant class, an impressive change of habits has occurred over the years. They direct more thought to private goals, including the accumulation of wealth, at the expense of concern for the public good or for society as an interdependent system. There has been a loss of a sense of a social contract. In tune with this mindset, public policies have facilitated a great upward transfer of wealth, through a systematic decrease in the tax burden imposed on the wealthiest sectors, and a huge national indebtedness.

Ultimately all major collective problems—the contamination of the environment, the ageing of infrastructure, the retirement system, public health, and debt servicing—have been deferred, passed from the present to the future, from those living today to those who will live tomorrow. It is not just a matter of policy, but it is a moral dilemma as well. Policies that concentrate wealth and defer problems to the future go against a basic principle of human development—an ethical standard that means something more than living one's own life to the fullest (in itself a highly commendable aim); that means making sure that those who come after us on the road of life will live as well as, or better than, us. From an economic point of view, this goal has a name: sustainability. From a moral point of view: intergenerational solidarity. They are two strands of the same rope that has been strained to the breaking point.

For Latin Americans, who were never too strong in economic matters, material development seldom held pride of place in the concert of values. In the North, under the influence of the Protestant ethic, economic activity had a different ethical meaning—not as subordinate value but as a value in itself. But in both contexts, North and South, economic categories were linked—albeit in different ways—to moral concepts. With the passage of time, this linkage was forgotten. Adam Smith, modern economy's founder, did not teach economic science in his native Scotland. He lectured in moral philosophy. He did not believe his best work to be *The Wealth of Nations*, which made him famous, but a treaty he titled *The Theory of Moral Sentiments*. Following Smith's classic views, we can say that "investing" means "giving something to the future." By contrast, running into debt implies "taking something away from the future." We can see a moral dilemma cropping up right away from this basic economic conceptual opposition. The current crisis is not just a technical breakdown; it is a crisis of profligacy—as in the expression "moral hazard." National debt is, after all, a collective swindle of the future to live in the here and now. Borrowing to consume is stealing one's later prospects and also those of one's descendants.

Today we have come to the end of a great illusion: living on borrowed money on the basis of a fictitious capital. Credit cards have hit a limit, mortgages have to be repaid, houses are worth less than what was borrowed to buy them, foreigners are reluctant to lend in exchange for treasury bonds because they receive promissory notes in devalued currency. In addition, two wars of attrition demand immense resources. The crisis is a reckoning.[9] But it is also an opportunity. Above all, it is the chance to have a great collective awakening. That is why in the middle of a crisis, many who were living in concealment or bad faith, could now deep down feel liberated. A hard truth provokes catharsis. The catharsis starts by acknowledging that countries—from the most powerful to the least powerful—make progress with an educated, skilled and dignified work force; with a high level of investment in infrastructure and technology that may secure a long employment chain; and with a fair and progressive tax system that may actually gather the funds required to pay for necessary government services. After so many years of wild illusions, some view this prospect as a "rude awakening." But it is not necessarily so. All things considered, this awakening is part of another dream: a healthy dream, one that has always been known as the American dream, but which is, deep down, a more universal one.

As the economic crisis unfolds internationally, I have *déjà vu*, a sense of reliving what I experienced in Argentina in 2001: total financial breakdown, and the collapse of government,[10] resulting from years of excessive borrowing and spending without a corresponding increase in productivity and production, that ultimately led to sovereign default—at the time, the financial failure was the largest one in history. Walking in the streets of Buenos Aires in those days I felt the trauma and saw the disruption of life. I witnessed protests, lootings, and riots. At the same time I sensed a catharsis, as people came together and took charge. In factories abandoned by their owners, the workers took over and kept production going. People bartered goods and services, took care of one another's children, and shared food. In blocks of condominiums the neighbors coordinated essential services in assemblies and delegated tasks to small committees. For a moment, soviets of the middle class seemed to run the city. There was a feeling of loss and desolation, and yet, a strong determination to survive. Despite all the impoverishment and regression, in two years' time the country was on the mend, with elected officials, and a booming export trade. Even though there was no fundamental change in the political system and basic issues went unaddressed, there was a kind of resurrection. The catchword was no longer bankruptcy but resilience. Life had resumed after the default, and Argentina started to grow again.

What nobody knew at the moment of catastrophe in 2001 was that Argentina, with its bad policies, its profligacy, and its traumatic default, was the canary in a much bigger mine.

Chapter Two

THE TROUBLES AT THE CENTER

Pain and Innovation

The Chinese call it *Weiji*. In Mandarin the word denotes, from its first character, "crisis," and from the second character, "crucial or opportune moment." What opportunities appear in the present global economic crisis? What are the most promising solutions of the many that are being proposed? Under which cover or pretext will they be enacted? I risk a preliminary forecast: Do not expect the birth of a radical new model for the economy, but a new way of connecting its principal sectors. Synergy is appropriate as a name for these processes.

Just like with a coin the planetary crisis that engulfs us has two sides. On one side, "Tails"—where the actual value of the metal piece appears—is, in our case, negative values: employment, economic activity, profits, savings, stock values, available credit, exports, and so on. On the other side of the coin, "Heads" —usually depicting a bust of a president or monarch, a face or a figure of authority—we find a serious but hopeful countenance. The double-sided configuration is a very old numismatic convention. It makes one think about the predecessors of the current crisis.

The Great Depression of the thirties, which also began in the United States, was not only a period of hardship and unemployment—it was a fertile era for social innovation as well. As a response to the economic and social crises of that era, the government initiated a veritable cascade of novel programs and experiments. Many of them became, with the passage of time, solid institutions that have survived until today and which, in fact, are still preventing the current crisis from deepening further. Social Security (the national inter-generational retirement plan of the US), the Securities and Exchange Commission (a regulatory body for the more dynamic markets), unemployment insurance, and the Federal Deposit Insurance Corporation (which protects depositors from the failure of banks) are all social inventions designed to shelter individuals from catastrophic mishaps and the infirmity of old age, but also to organize the economic system in which the individuals interact.

These and other institutions were established to cushion the system from financial crashes that are usually followed by a deflationary spiral. Without them today the bank deposits of millions of citizens would be blocked or lost, unemployment would easily reach a level of 25 per cent or more, and retirees would lose their livelihood, their homes, their health, and what remains of their lives. In other words, without these buffer institutions established in the thirties, the United States and other advanced economies would have been in 2008–9 in a similar situation to that of Argentina in 2001–2. Other programs instituted in the thirties, such as the Work Projects Administration (WPA) and the National Recovery Administration (NRA) were terminated as soon as the economy showed signs of recovery at the end of that fateful decade.

Later I will consider the prospect for a repeat of the largest public works program of all—one that many argue pulled the American economy out of the Depression, namely, security preparedness and the mobilization for World War II. It would be absurd and even perverse to recommend a recurrence of that titanic *casus belli* in this century. Luckily, the type of postindustrial and globalized production of present-day economies prevents a mass mobilization of mid-twentieth century proportions. But we should not forget the fact that that large-scale war effectively got rid of the unrealized surplus of the economy, eliminated idle capacity in factories and enterprises of all kinds, fostered the full employment of the labor force, and ultimately made it possible for the United States to emerge from the conflict some 300 times richer than it was at the beginning; thereby assuring its world hegemony for the next fifty years. That experience cannot be repeated, and it is a good thing that it cannot be repeated. But many of the social, economic, and technological programs that will be set in motion in the coming years will need an international "security" legitimation to overcome ingrained social habits, vested interests, and ideological prejudices. They will represent a form of near-total social mobilization to face environmental risks and security threats in a world in which local crises easily metastasize into global emergencies. I will develop this argument in the section on the future of warfare.

The current consensus among economists (with all due reservations, since these persons have demonstrated a predictive acumen comparable to the reading of tea leaves) is that our global economy is not doomed to the same fate as the world economy of the thirties. Nevertheless, the collapse of the financial system and the freezing of credit are as real today as they were then. The trail of consequences is being felt in the "real" economy, and its impact has only begun. There will be more dramatic failures of enterprises and markets in the near future. Some of the symptoms are visible already: rising unemployment, consumer diffidence, mortgage foreclosures, and the imperative need of retirees to return to work—if they can find work—in order to make ends meet. Savings have evaporated; investments are stalled; and money, when available, is being hoarded rather than put to productive use.

Under such conditions, the public sector has moved from being a guarantor of last resort to being a first responder. The specter of socialism has returned to haunt the capitalist economy, not as a gravedigger but as a rescuer.

Longer-term initiatives are more difficult to fathom but they are even more important than emergency measures. There will be in the end at least a partial nationalization of the banking sector, a greater regulation of financial flows, a greater public control and accountability of private economic transactions, and a greater demand for public services—since demand for other goods and services has experienced a precipitous drop. There will also be a greater demand for services provided by the third sector, that is, nonprofit organizations from private foundations to churches and civil-society associations. But here again, and in a process similar to that of the private enterprise sector, we must expect a concentration and consolidation of resources.

It is astonishing to behold how governments that until recently professed a devout commitment to free unregulated markets are now intervening with force and gusto in the economy. They do not hesitate to launch programs that hitherto they would have denounced as bordering on collectivism. Robust state intervention has ceased to be a bad word, at least in some sectors. In the United States alone the Bush administration (never suspected of socialist leanings) turned its policies 180 degrees on a number of fronts from bailouts to direct state control of economic enterprises in particular to financial and insurance companies assistance—with such strings attached as government-mandated limits to CEO compensation. These are hard times, indeed, when a right-wing Republican administration feels compelled to take measures that are more in tune with "national and popular" regimes in other parts of the world.

At the state and local level, authorities also took measures that were unusual and radical in the American context. The sheriff of County Cook, in Chicago, for example issued an order to his deputies not to enforce home foreclosures, and to leave families in their places of residence that they could no longer afford. Of course nobody knows if all these measures and gestures will stop the decline in economic activity. So far, from the top of the federal administration down to local authorities those in charge are improvising, playing it by ear.

We have entered an era of fear and uncertainty. People begin searching for "out-of-the-box" solutions of proven responses. New ideas on how to work, how to use transport, how to consume energy, and how to govern communities are already appearing in articles, editorials, think-tank proposals, and government task force reports. In many corners of the globe, from China to Latin America to Europe and Africa, people are experimenting how to live better with less. In many parts of the world, the public asks what is the proper role of governments? What is the social responsibility of enterprises? What is the proper role for NGOs? We are moving from the narcissistic absorption with private troubles to a debate on public issues. The time has come for many people to consider the meaning of economic success, for questioning the underlying values of hitherto unexamined pursuits. What is freedom, especially economic freedom? Until recently our economic understanding was that it was freedom from regulation and public intervention, but we did not ask what purpose freedom serves in a social world that is not just a sum of its parts. Can the market alone provide us with health, education, and well-being? What are the different meanings of "the pursuit of happiness"?

The answers to these and related questions will not necessarily lead to a revamped New Deal. The experience of the last half-century has shown that the responsibility to solve social problems does not rest exclusively on the shoulders of government. But more recent experiences have demonstrated that the private sector can also fail, and fail quite miserably.

What I see in front of us is a new pact among the public, the private, and the non-governmental or third sectors of society. Each sector has some answers to our plight but not one of them has all the answers. There are no monolithic solutions to the crisis. The challenge is to know who does what best, and how to combine the diverse strands of excellence.[1] This art of combination and collaboration between countervailing groups is the art of synergy.

Crisis as Provocation

A great crisis is also an opportunity to institute reforms that ground an economy on a more sustainable basis. It is precisely that that is at stake right now in the United States after a truly historic presidential election. The global capitalist system with its base in the United States has not been vanquished—though it is, indeed, in danger. Nonetheless, it is a system that boasts sizeable reserves, enormous advantages, and a historical capacity to bet big. The time for new and radical state policies is upon us. Will the new government be up to the task? Is the American political system sufficiently functional to accept and digest serious reforms?

"You will see things, friend Sancho, that will make stones speak." Don Quixote was right. As I noted in the previous chapter, the twenty-first century's global capitalist crisis has given rise to a kind of rescue socialism, backed by the loftiest members of the global elite. And something very serious must be happening when orthodox economists start talking like Hegelian philosophers.[2]

Indeed, the president of the World Bank, the very technical and sensible Mr. Robert B. Zoellick, argued in an article published in *The Washington Post* that a world in crisis offers, in turn, a chance for greatness.[3] Thesis: a capitalism dominated by the financial sector, without limits or restraints; Antithesis: a catastrophic crisis; Synthesis: a new, happier world, reorganized by strong and rational leaders and built around a healthier economy. It makes sense to take a closer look at this dialectic that shows some optimism in place of the usual doom. Hegel himself said that the most sublime concepts are fruits of existence and that the nature of existence is overcoming pain.

The first proof is easy. As increasing numbers of enterprises go bankrupt, or as the financial/real estate crisis impacts the "real economy," given the general impotence of banks and multinational organizations the tendency is to regulate markets, nationalize businesses, and move closer toward protectionism—that is some form of economic nationalism. While these trends may manifest themselves differently in diverse countries and regions, the conclusion is clear: the neoliberal model is, beyond a shadow of a doubt, a thing of the past. It has been replaced—silently, without preaching or ideological proclamations—by a pragmatic model, in essence a "Chinese" one (in the sense of Deng Xiao Ping's program) that nationalizes and regulates but falls short of constructing a planned economy. Just as the neoliberal model generated a real revolution in the planetary division of labor—but a revolution built on a weak and speculative foundation—so too, the new model may create a new order and a new equilibrium, built on a more sustainable foundation that will make possible a new era of accumulation.

The second proof is more difficult because it runs counter to common sense or, better put, counter to today's hysteria. There are those who claim that the crisis marks the end of American hegemony and that US-style capitalism will now be obliged to share power and profits with emerging and resurgent world powers: the BRICs, Europe, and perhaps other countries rich in natural and energy resources. This claim is not completely erroneous. Comparative social indicators show the US at a disadvantage relative to other countries and even to its own past prosperity in terms of health, education, social protection, transport, environmental stewardship, and infrastructure. This is the consequence of a quarter-century of neglecting its own social and human capital while shifting the bulk of industrial production to other continents and compensating for it with deficit spending and speculation. As I tried to show in the first chapter, this was the great illusion of "easy money" (in the Argentina of the 1970s the speculative mania was called *plata dulce*, "sweet cash")[1]: economic growth sustained through massive consumption on credit "guaranteed" by a spurious assessment of property values. The current crisis is nothing more that the dramatic and painful correction of the excesses of that phase of accumulation. But the crisis need not represent a terminal condition, provided that conditions for a strategic exit are fulfilled.

Contrary to the titles screaming from the shelves of bookstores, this crisis cannot be compared to the fall of the old Roman Empire. A "Roman" collapse occurs when a system expands too much and wanders dangerously far from its base. It is then attacked from the periphery and retreats, until finally the "barbarians" (those from the outside) seize the center and destroy it. In other words, it is an exogenic and centripetal process. The current global crisis, on the other hand, is endogenic and centrifugal: It began in the center of the system, contaminated the immediate surroundings, and produced the most harmful effects on the extreme periphery. This insight helps to make sense of the fact that, in the middle of the American collapse, governments and investors around the world still line up to buy dollars rather than turning to other currencies. In this so-called "fall" of the American empire, the "barbarians" are not besieging the Capitol but are seeking refuge there. What is the magic power of the dollar even in its decline? Why, instead of repelling, does America attract so many foreigners—above all the governments of those countries that are supposedly standing in line to replace the United States as the dominant power?

Ever since the famous decoupling of the dollar from the value of gold, which President Nixon effected in 1971, the world has lived with a flexible, or floating, dollar. During the seventies, the United States became the financial center of the world. After the gold standard ended the Federal Reserve— the US central bank—proceeded to issue the national currency, without any backing in precious metals, as an international currency. Since then the Federal Reserve has regulated international interest rates and issued Treasury bonds that function as the true backing for the global dollar. This has enabled the United States to amass a foreign debt in its very own currency—a privilege that no other country has secured and one that is almost inconceivable. Today nearly all American liabilities for goods and services are owed in dollars. It is the only truly "bullet-proof" system in the world.

The system creates a tremendous asymmetry between the external exposure of the United States and the exposure of other countries.[5] As Latin Americans who have suffered repeated foreign debt crises know all too well, financial obligations must be paid in the currencies of others. The US, however, pays its debts by printing green bills. It is the only case of a country capable of determining the interest rate on its own foreign debt. To reprise my earlier argument, this system in question is circular, centrifugal, and nearly unbeatable. Even the world's biggest creditor, the People's Republic of China—which boasts international reserves of more than 2 trillion dollars—has to play by this system's rules. I will only be convinced of the end of American hegemony when this circular, dollar-based system is replaced by other reference currencies. And this seems unlikely for quite some time.[6]

Now it should be clearer why the dollar system is centrifugal: It distributes the crisis from the inside to the outside, from the center to the margins and, at the same time, prevents the unexpected breakage of the bonds of globalization. It is a system in which the creditor is at the mercy of the debtor. This enables the system, currently in crisis mode, to rebalance itself without a precipitous loss of hegemony, provided that there is strategic management from the centers of power.

Continuing with the example of China as a creditor tied to the prow of the American debtor, the rebalancing act will be achieved through the accelerated development of the creditor's domestic market, with greater domestic consumption and a progressive lessening of the need to invest reserves in the American debt. For the United States this same process may afford the time needed to make significant investments—many of them "socialized"—in new, cutting-edge technology, with an emphasis on "green" machinery, and in the modernization of infrastructure and human capital. On the other hand, if for internal reasons—like political gridlock – the US fails to reform, then its decline will commence in earnest.

Over the medium range (investments that see returns after 15 or 20 years) this strategy could drive a new cycle of growth, which would be less speculative and based more on technical and scientific content than on financial content. In other words, growth will owe less to vendor finance of exports and more to social inclusion and internal prosperity. Provided there is effective management of public policy and a good sense of strategy, this new model of accumulation should arrive just in time to address intelligently and productively (rather than merely defensively) the environmental challenges that loom over a planet—that, in a few decades time, will be home to 9.2 billion people.

To repeat, the current global crises originate with the hegemonic power. They are crises of exuberance and not of anemia. In crises like these, the system "suspends" its own rules and ideology while it readjusts—ideally to reemerge as the engine that drives the growth of other countries engaged in the global economy. Any assessment of the leadership of a world power must take into account more than good times of growth and expansion. It must also consider the intensity of its nation's "pain," as Hegel would say, and, ultimately, the speed of its recovery.

The 2008 presidential election in the US was the first test of the country's capacity for recovery through means that are unorthodox and novel, i.e., experimental. New and radical measures are precisely those that no one wants to take during "normal times." In "normal times" major political players and interest groups have the power to veto audacious policies and even those state policies that do not bear fruit within the short election cycle. But during "times of great crisis" the game changes.

The main political actors become paralyzed and the big interest groups find themselves in need of help. These times amount to a true "state of exception" and endow the ruling power a freedom of action otherwise inconceivable. For example, consider that during the Great Depression of the 1930s, President Roosevelt enacted the era's most daring (i.e., "socialist") policies during the span of only 100 days.[7]

The time has come for a significant change in America's ruling team, which is, for the moment, the world's ruling team. Though it began in the financial sector, the crisis is already generating a global deflationary tendency, i.e., a true depression. The coming changes will be painful. The ruling team must adopt mid-range and long-term state policies, the only kind of policies suitable for cultivating sustained global leadership over the course of the next century. The president must rise above the two traditional parties and launch, with the backing of a good team, his own reform program. Whereas the president may himself be up to the challenge the other political forces may not. The two parties only offer the platitudes of tired men and women. They are tired to lead, but not tired enough to block necessary reforms. If as a result the country drifts, a period of political instability may well follow, with faint echoes of Latin America. The crisis may then move from Wall Street to Washington, DC. The American political system may then move from the state of exceptional stability, to which it is accustomed, to a true state of exception.[8]

Spurious Socialism to the Rescue

The great global crisis that began in the United States with the burst of the real estate bubble has required the state to quasi-nationalize large financial enterprises and socialize losses. This amounts to a kind of top-down, rescue socialism. We cannot be sure if these measures will suffice to cure capitalism of its excesses but it does seem like a new world order is taking shape, one where socialism complements capitalism.

When the Soviet Union collapsed, taking with it a model of state socialism that had nourished the hopes of many during the twentieth century, a Russian sociologist friend made the following comment, which I shall always remember, "The Cold War was a tango between two dancers. One of them has fallen. When do you think the other's time will come?" It was not clear if he was referring to Russia and the United States or to the systems that each represented: communism and liberalism—or, if you prefer, communism and capitalism. Confronted with this quandary, I responded with another question, perhaps tinged with sarcasm, "In your opinion, was it communism that ruined Russia or Russia that ruined communism?" To this day neither my friend nor anyone else has offered satisfactory answers to either of these questions. Nonetheless, twenty years after the end of the Cold War, the US economy is experiencing a crisis whose severity has put in jeopardy the entire capitalist system.

The world has not seen a similar collapse since the Great Depression of the 1930s. Just as during that era, confidence in the munificence of capitalism is losing ground day by day. It remains to be seen whether the root of the crisis lies with the heretofore-hegemonic power's mismanagement of the economy (in other words, whether the crisis owes to a peculiarity of what the Europeans call America's "wild capitalism") or whether the problem is inherent in capitalism itself, beyond all national idiosyncrasies. In any case, it is little use speculating about the origins of the outbreak when it has already reached epidemic proportions. Just as in the 1930s, today there are voices clamoring for swift and energetic state intervention. But the analogy ends there.

In contrast to the 1930s when communism was still in its adolescence (it had already shown signs of brutality but not yet of serious inefficiency), today no one is seriously proposing alternatives to the reigning economic system. Since the eighties when Margaret Thatcher and Ronald Reagan proselytized the virtues of economic liberalism—a philosophy which Thatcher synthesized in the acronym TINA (There is no alternative)—and which, over the subsequent two decades, elites in the East and the West and in both the Northern and Southern Hemispheres internalized, no other economic model has proven viable.

There have been, without a doubt, reactions against the excesses of neoliberalism in those Southern countries that experienced severe crises and then experimented with state policies quite distinct from those once extolled by advocates of the "Washington Consensus." Nonetheless, in my opinion, these oppositional policies are, in fact, parasitic: dependent on the smooth functioning of global capitalism in the great centers of economic growth. These experiments—whether called socialist, populist, or nationalist—have depended on markets for their natural resources, in particular, energy and commodities.[9] There is no geostrategic equivalence between the nationalizing and redistributive polices of those countries that export oil, gas or soy, for example, and the inverse historical movement, i.e., the transition from a state socialist model to a capitalist market model that has been underway in the People's Republic of China since the rule of Deng Xiao Ping.[10]

But now the kind of crisis that once affected only peripheral countries, the so-called "emerging markets," has turned its fury on the very center of the system. In order to rescue this system, the principal managers of global capitalism—political leaders, central bank officials, treasurers, and large investors—are recurring to any and all state instruments at their disposal. In short, capitalism's own elites want the state to take responsibility for unpayable debts, bankrupt banks, depreciated titles, and devalued capital goods that the free market itself cannot absorb without risking paralysis. Put simply, they want to socialize the market losses.

Many years ago, the celebrated economist, John Kenneth Galbraith, declared, with customary flair, "In America, the only respectable type of socialism is socialism for the rich." Just a few years after his death, this prophetic declaration is being fulfilled. It would seem that the twenty-first century socialism in the North is not Bolivarian but Washingtonian: It is not an egalitarian socialism but rather a kind of financial, rescue socialism. This brand of socialism does not go about shirtless and in workboots; it wears Zegna suits and Ferragamo shoes.

So far the United States has presented to the world a drama in several acts, the first of which has just closed. What made the drama especially compelling was the concurrence of the financial crisis and a presidential election. In one of many episodes of political theater, we saw the defeated-looking president Bush meet with his two potential successors as well as with congressional leaders from both parties and an entourage of state officials—all of them with brows furrowed, reciting grave warnings about the pressing need to act during a state of emergency. The names of these officials have become global public knowledge, as if they were Hollywood stars or soccer players: besides Mr. Bush, whose name is already fading into the past, the protagonists included Hank Paulsen, Ben Bernanke, Nancy Pelosi, Harry Reid, and, of course, the then candidates Barack Obama and John McCain. At that stage of the game, their message was plain: "We need to immediately approve a rescue plan so the state can buy, with taxpayer money, the bad titles and stocks that are currently paralyzing credit and, in turn, all of economic activity." The words reminded me of those of the Argentine nineteenth-century statesman Domingo F. Sarmiento, "When it comes to governing, things need to get done, whether it be well or poorly." Those who are interested in political theory will remember arguments in favor of a state of emergency expounded by advocates of fisted rule from Thomas Hobbes to Carl Schmitt.

Nonetheless, rescue socialism, or, if ones prefers, the respectable intervention in the marketplace by the respected Treasury Secretary and ex-CEO of Goldman Sachs, Henry Paulsen, with the aid of Chairman of the Federal Reserve Ben Bernanke, a respected former economist from Princeton and expert in, of all things, the Great Depression of the 1930s, met with stiff resistance in the House of Representatives, where the rescue plan was initially blocked by a thin margin. This rejection came not from what passes in the US as the "left," i.e., the liberal wing of the Democratic party, but from the right wing of the Republican party, then the ruling party. The message was as clear as it was extreme: Let the market take responsibility for its own errors. The state must remain strictly out of the equation. This argument repeated nearly verbatim recommendations given by another treasury secretary, Andrew Mellon, in response to the bank crisis of 1929–1932. He offered this advice: Liquidate, liquidate. In other words, may those who deserve to go broke, go broke. What happened next is a piece of history: the six-year Great Depression. Eventually, someone convinced the resisting representatives that a serious leak threatens to sink the whole ship and that those who do not learn from history are doomed to repeat it. A modified rescue package passed a new vote and was approved on October 3, 2008. We will come to remember this date as the birthday of rescue socialism.

The new American-style socialism is the work of a pragmatic, capitalist elite. Suspicion and resistance spring from several sources: popular segments who still adhere to extreme market fundamentalism, as well as broader segments who see their retirement assets dwindling and their jobs threatened, who have less and less buying power, who fear getting sick because they are uninsured, and who hold out little hope of progress for their children and grandchildren. As the crisis evolves, it is possible that resistance to "Wall Street greed" will migrate from its right-wing populist base and re-center itself in more progressive circles. But this is not certain.

Complicating the current economic crisis is a simultaneous crisis of leadership. After certain concessions, a bipartisan coalition of party elites initiated a rescue plan with hopes of gaining a little breathing room until after the elections. Only after the election, and after the first year of the new administration are we able to begin to gauge the longer-term prospects of the global system after its reform, and the geostrategic re-composition of the planet. It is important now, however, to survey those prospects and to ask what role the Southern countries will play after this crisis is over.

After spending a quarter century trying to dismantle state machinery and to vilify state intervention in the economy, big capitalism—in response to a huge financial stumble and the first great crisis of globalization—has turned to the state for salvation. But it finds a state with precious little management capacity. During Bush's presidency, the US has proven dreadfully ineffective at fighting wars (the occupation of Iraq and the war in Afghanistan offer resounding proof), at mobilizing resources in the wake of natural disasters (the destruction of New Orleans by Hurricane Katrina and more recently the BP oil spill in the Gulf of Mexico are indications that the problem is systemic and beyond the scope of a single administration), at rationally limiting spending, at providing healthcare, and at many other undertakings. In the wake of desperate measures represented by the current rescue package, the firm hand of a true reformist—someone along the lines of a Franklin Delano Roosevelt—will be needed to rebuild the state. So far, all hands at the helm seem shaky.

At this stage in history socialism is not a viable global alternative to capitalism, but it seems increasingly evident that socialism does provide a necessary complement. While capitalism may be the locomotive of growth and prosperity, it falls to socialism to provide the tracks on which this engine runs. A bullet train without tracks is bound to derail. In 1990 a financial crisis— similar to that afflicting the US right now—occurred in Sweden, a corner of the world with little geopolitical repercussion. But the example remains relevant. In the case of Sweden, the state came to the rescue with swift and effective socialist-type interventions. And now for many years Sweden has complemented its vigorous capitalist economy with socialist measures. Has the time come to reconsider the Scandinavian model? A little Swedish could help. *Jag talar och skriver liten svenska.*[11] However, deep cultural differences remain: In a pinch, the Swedes had the government take over the banks. In a pinch, the Americans let the bankers take over the government.

The Fading Remedies of War

The function of war in the recovery from depression has long been a subject of debate ever since a faltering New Deal was rebooted by preparedness and military action. War, like the weather is forever with us and always changes.

"Marlborough has left for the war" is one of the most popular folk songs in the French and Spanish languages. English speakers will immediately recognize the tune in the well-known song *"For he's a jolly good fellow."* It is the burlesque lament for the presumed death of John Churchill, first Duke of Marlborough, in the battle of Malplaquet in 1709. Today's Marlborough leaves for a new type of war.

When Al Qaeda attacked the U.S. homeland on September 11, 2001, it hit two of the three seemingly intended targets: Wall Street and The Pentagon (it also aimed possibly at the Capitol Building or the White House). In doing so, however, the non-state organization hit neither nerve nor muscle, but symbol and fat. As Michel Foucault said many years ago, power does not reside in institutions with a fixed address but in networks and relations. It did succeed, however, in shocking the world with a bloody and spectacular publicity stunt, and it managed to bait the most powerful nation into declaring a "war on terror," which distorted the meaning of the first noun beyond recognition. Latin Americans, like everybody else, were shocked by the spectacle, and surmised that something fundamental had changed in the world. But nobody knew how the effects would ripple and events would unfold.

Blinded by the sneak attack, the United States reacted like the giant Polyphemus when wily Odysseus and his itinerant crew struck him. It embarked upon a conventional war of choice against the wrong target: a dilapidated third-rate power that soon morphed into a protracted site of unconventional violence. Unprepared for the latter, the occupying nation managed it so poorly that in the end the largest power on earth jeopardized the armed forces, lost prestige, and drained the treasury. Several hundred thousand troops in rotation, "network-centric" warfare with space-age technology, pilotless aircraft, precision-guided munitions, and a budget upwards of 400 billion dollars have had a hard time managing 20 to 30 thousand insurgents armed with simple or improvised lethal devices, who choose where to strike and how.

The 9/11 attack and its aftermath—especially the fiasco of Iraq—forced into the open a realization that had been gaining ground among serious military analysts and historians, but which had remained largely hidden from the public in developed societies, namely, that the classical notions of strategy taught for generations in military schools were woefully inadequate to deal with the realities of twenty-first century conflicts.

War, as we have come to know it in the period between 1648 and 1945, is ever more manifestly an obsolescent institution. Others more capable than I have analyzed this evolution or involution into near-extinction.[12] As is often the case with declining institutions, its specific defeasance is marked by the abusive extension of the word to cover metaphorically very different phenomena. We have had a war on drugs, a war on poverty, and of course, the war on terror. We may soon add to the list of *guerres du jour* a war on economic depression. The targets are the windmills of Don Quixote.

At the same time, both rich and developing nations insist on procuring weapons systems that are exquisite, expensive, and largely useless, and on maintaining military establishments whose main role in "low-intensity" conflicts that rage around the world is that of "observers" and "peace keepers"— impotent before civil wars, insurgencies, ethnic cleansings, and genocides.

Non-state actors wage war against each other and against organized states. As the cities of New York, Madrid, London, and Mumbai know, these actors are no longer kept outside the gates of the "civilized." Like other global networks, terrorist organizations no longer respect borders, civilian/military distinctions, or transcendent symbols.

There is therefore a serious disconnect between the new challenges and the conventional responses. Most defense establishments are beholden to the realities and the ideas of yesteryear while violent conflicts of a different kind multiply like maggots in the bodies of failed or weakening states. Do these conflicts merit the label of "war"? One is hesitant to employ the word after it has been subjected to so much abuse. However, we may keep it if we also keep in mind at least the following features: first, it is organized violence waged by non-state actors; second, it confounds civilian and military distinctions; third, it is global (it knows neither physical nor symbolic borders); and fourth, it is more expressive than instrumental (more an end than a means). Standing before this reality, the world of *Realpolitik*—a bunch of nation-states claiming a monopoly of legitimate violence over fixed territories and fighting over their respectively perceived interests—must adapt both adequately and fast, or it will sink into irrelevance. This is easier said than done. The old aggregates persist; military-industrial complexes are hard to reform and redirect. Above all, mindsets are hard to change.

And yet, a window for reform is now opening with the global economic crisis. After years of unfettered growth in military budgets, not only in the extant superpower—the United States—but also in China and in resurgent Russia, as well as in aspiring regional powers (whose military ambitions are often fueled by petro-dollars) the sharp global economic downturn will have a serious impact on weapons procurement. In the United States alone, the Pentagon's annual base budget for standard operations has reached half a trillion dollars, the highest since World War II. And this excludes investment in new weapons. The question is no longer whether large defense budgets will break the bank, but how to manage military expenses after the bank is broke. And behind these queries looms the biggest question of all: What is the role of war preparedness in the large public works programs that are needed to jump start stalled economies?

Across the military services, meetings behind closed doors are devoted to figuring out where and how to cut spending. Therefore, this is a moment of rare candor in the military establishments. Beyond the dilemma of cutting here or there, muscle or fat, the more important issue is how to redesign and redirect the whole expenditure effort so that it is more rational and useful and less inertial and useless.

At the moment, the most likely targets for cuts are likely to be the expensive, super-sophisticated arms programs that constitute the theoretical pride of a super-power. Given my argument before, this is all for the good. Weapons systems are to our societies what pyramids were to the Egyptians. In the United States, some of these programs have had cost overruns estimated in the hundreds of billions. As a result the US Congressional watchdog offices are poised to reduce spending for advanced combat systems, and such jewels of the arsenal as the Air Force's Joint Strike Fighter, the Navy's latest-designed destroyers, and the very missile defense system that has soured relations between the US and the Russian Federation. The time has arrived to ask what purpose do these weapons systems serve, and even whether they have any manifest purpose at all. The other big ticket in military expense, also outside the budget for standard operations, is the "supplemental" spending for the wars in Iraq and Afghanistan, which is running in excess of $100 billion a year. The central fact about these wars is that, despite the enormous resources thrown at them, they never have come near to what even remotely could be defined as "victory" for the powers that wage them. Contrary to politicians back home, no responsible commander in the field uses the term.

The asymmetry between expense and "payoff" also prompts doubts, in these times, about the functionality, sense, and purpose of war as we have known throughout the ages. In short, both high-tech in the skies and boots on the ground do not seem to do the job they are supposed to do.

What, therefore, is to be done? The first job is to recognize that the challenges are complicated—a puzzle of pre-modern violence and post-modern networks. The second job is to acknowledge that all military establishments—and preeminently that of the extant superpower—are not equipped for the task. The Pentagon does not have enough troops and equipment to remain in Iraq and fight in Afghanistan, let alone to face additional crises elsewhere, should they break out. If 663.8 billion dollars (the budget for 2010) cannot do the job, what will? Having other nations—actual and potential allies—add their resources to the pot will not help: their combined defense budgets are smaller than the single American budget. One cannot keep feeding a dinosaur.

It is clear that it is not an issue of resources but of design. The third job therefore is to rebuild and reshape the military establishments to face elusive enemies and disparate dangers, which morph like retroviruses. As Ulrich Beck has proposed,[13] we are in a global risk society and no longer exclusively in a system of states. What remains of the this system of states is itself evolving with the emergence of regional powers such as China, Russia, India, Iran, and Brazil; with the instability—and therefore unpredictability—of other significant nations like Pakistan and North Korea (significant insofar as they have a limited nuclear capability); and, finally, with a number of failed or failing smaller states. Conventional wars, and even a nuclear one, may yet break out in the rimland states.[14] On this geopolitical fault line containment and deterrence are essential, aggression and confrontation a mistake. NATO and the United States must devise a strategy to keep these state actors in check. The one lesson of Iraq is that preemptive wars of choice are likely to turn into strategic disasters because they breed a different type of challenge, namely, insurgencies, where the odds of "winning" are low. Moreover preemptive doctrines set a dangerous precedent: if one state launches one such war, others will feel equally entitled. That is a sure path to Armageddon. One lesson of Iraq is that nation busting followed by (usually botched) nation building is putting the cart before the horse. In the end, strategic retreat and increased diplomacy were required. Paradoxical as it may sound, such strategic retreat will result in the regrouping, repair, retraining, and even the enlargement of the ground forces.

The biggest challenge is of a different order, though related to the evolving system of states. It has appeared in its crevices and will continue to grow. It is by no means new, but has acquired a new significance. It goes by the names of irregular warfare, insurgency, or the far less apt one of "terror."

As Martin van Creveld has observed in several books on the transformation of warfare, manuals on counter-insurgency fill entire libraries, but most should be discarded, for the simple reason that they have been written by the losing side. To date there is no silver bullet in this type of war: the two or three success stories since 1945 are very context-specific and disallow sweeping generalizations. The lessons learned are somewhat modest and few. Moreover, they are at opposite poles of the spectrum: from swift and brutal suppression to slow and patient reconciliation. One thing, however, is clear: this kind of warfare has as much to do with intelligence gathering, police operations, and social science understanding (from anthropology to economics and political sociology) as with killing the enemy.

What we are likely to see in the near future in the United States is the interpenetration of military and civilian programs, and the militarization of foreign aid and poverty reduction—in the words of the president of the World Bank Robert B. Zoellick, "bringing security and development together." Given the financial crisis and the ensuing long depression that has engulfed the world, homeland and international security will be the mantle under which new public works projects will be undertaken. Just as war preparedness was the public works projects that finally pulled the United States out of the Great Depression, so will an updated type of war preparedness help pull our globalized economy out of the doldrums. But it will not be mass industrial production for a titanic combat—Rosie the Riveter helping produce 100,000 combat planes a year—but a different sort of mobilization, aimed at conflict prevention, poverty reduction, and the propping of failed states. Just as the Pentagon will become partially a development agency, so will civil society (thousands of civilian experts and volunteers) be summoned to collaborate in the containment of new wars. These will include economists, public administrators, public health experts, agronomists, city planners, social anthropologists, political scientists, and sociologists. And just as there will be a certain "civilianization" of the armed forces, so will there be new militarized civilian agencies like the proposed Civilian Reserve Corps.

The new Pentagon and its counterparts elsewhere will focus less on classic war toys (like blue water fighting vessels, aerial combat fighters that play war games with each other for lack of serious enemies, or untested missile defense systems) and more on coastal, transport, and lift capacity to deploy huge quantities of armed personnel and equipment from one emergency in a corner of the world to another. Other nations, including the United Nations, will join in a secondary and support capacity. The Americans will provide the muscle for heavy lifting; the others the softer power of skills and expert assistance.

War yields fewer and different dividends today. However, war will be with us until the end of time, not because of deep psychological drives as

Freud thought, but largely for sociological reasons: it is an extreme sport for which there are no real substitutes. But its shape has changed enormously. Classic "trinitarian" war[15] is dead; titanic world wars have passed; doomsday thermonuclear exchange is over. The wars that will remain are the following: occasional conventional wars in the rimland; potentially a regional nuclear exchange; here and there localized insurgencies in failed states; and last but not least, terrorist attacks *urbi et orbi*—poising networks of organized states against networks of non-state subversives. The price to be paid for defense in these wars is ever more intrusive surveillance of civil societies with the ensuing paradox: the more developed a society the more subject to surveillance. In these new guises war will continue to stalk humanity, and peace will be as elusive as always.

Peace has no heroes. In *extremis* it produces martyrs. The original meaning of this term (in Greek μάρτυς) placed it at the opposite pole of combat: not to bear arms, but to bear witness. From Jesus to Ghandi, a great many charismatic figures that have advocated peace met a violent end. It was perhaps the cruelty of their denouement that helped preserve their memory. The social movements that followed the nonviolent example of those charismatic types have interpreted the latter's tragic demise as an act of sacrifice. But the sanctification by blood brings them back full circle to their archetypical nemesis: the warriors.

Latin Americans should heed these developments in the North, and draw some conclusions for their region. Although hot wars in the classic mode are gone, military preparedness is not. It has morphed into a flexible and diverse mobilization in pursuit of elusive targets. Preparedness blurs the distinction between civilians and warriors in a web of high-tech information. Security and intelligence prevail over weaponry. This system of preparedness is useful for R&D (research and development, which entails education) and employment, and disciplines—in subtle and non-subtle ways—the population. It helps an advanced society keep the technological edge. It generates both hardware and organizational products that everybody else will adopt and consume. The exception to this discussion is hostile regimes. They produce and consume their own security—evolved from Eastern Europe in the totalitarian era. Their systems of surveillance and repressive action are efficient and in some cases more advanced than those in the West because they form part of the DNA of the regimes. The interpenetration of the intelligence and security apparatus of Cuba and Venezuela is a laboratory of this rival set of controls. Military business will continue to matter. They cannot be disentangled from the global risk society. On a more parochial level we should not underestimate the convenience of saber rattling to holders of power as a dangerous game designed to distract and to channel discontent.

Chapter Three

THE RESPONSE

What the South Can Tell the North

As the crisis first loomed and then broke out, the US presidential campaign raised an important question for that country and for the world: in view of the multiple problems hovering over it, was American society willing to accept a cast generational change and a shift in course regarding state policies? The election was between fear and hope. Seen from the Latin American experience, the election gave the crisis in the North another face—an opportunity for action that would be less conditioned by the restraints of the recent past and the outgoing administration.

The great changes in social, economic and political direction in Latin America in the last decades have been propelled less by a plan, a will agreed by consensus, or a coherent ideology than by the harsh necessity and the strong and recurrent crises that have shaken the continent. Those crises, and their respective exits, have had both good and adverse effects. A sign of discontinuity thus characterizes recent Latin American history. Therefore, there has been neither sustained economic development nor systematic social progress.

To simplify, I will say that the last decades' great Latin American crises have been two: the first one was the hyperinflationary crisis of the eighties, which marked the exhaustion of a substitutive industrial development style, mainly geared to domestic markets. To get out of that crisis, government elites were forced to change course dramatically with respect to prior public policies and accepted new recipes for stabilization, privatization, and opening-up to a new global world. That 180-degree change was labeled "neoliberal." The remedy, adopted with haste and administered in overdoses, worked for a while but had very harmful side effects: de-industrialization, unemployment, increase in poverty and inequality, and the growth of a large informal sector, among others. In some countries like Argentina and Ecuador, the strategy led to an intolerable debt increase and to national bankruptcy.[1]

After a decade of neoliberal policies a new crisis cropped up—this time deflationary in nature—that was experienced in some countries as an outbreak of a terminal disease: the arrival at the top of disheveled states new government casts who were ready to adopt urgent rescue measures and to try other exits. Default, devaluation, nationalizations, more state interference in the market, and attempts at income redistribution were some of these measures. Most of these governments defined themselves as "leftist," using quite an open and sometimes contradictory meaning of the venerable term, whose semantics has been reduced in the last 25 years to policies that seek to produce greater social equality and greater inclusion of marginalized groups as well as more ideological independence from the traditional institutions of the North—but without offering convincing alternatives to the standard practices in global markets.

For reasons that I find difficult to understand, in Latin America there is a manifest tendency to pack policies and assign them a systematic quality they really do not have. Thus, the measures adopted by many governments in the eighties and nineties are interpreted as a logical result of a conspiracy and disastrous plan, an entelechy called "neoliberalism" which is given the title of "model." Likewise, but with an opposite intention, the measures taken by many current governments are interpreted as a part of a different "model," sometimes called "a developmental state," "the third way" or, more solemnly, "twenty-first-century socialism." Yet, a calm analysis leads to a different conclusion: the so-called "models" are only emergency packages whose aim is to get out of a crisis. To render a Spanish saying in English: the flailing of arms of someone who is drowning is not a swimming style.[2]

Lessons to Learn

It is not my purpose here to analyze Latin American governments' public policies of the last 20 or 30 years. My aim is to introduce a topic that I believe is an important lesson that Latin America's recent history provides: the role crises play in the adoption of strong and necessary measures—but very difficult to carry out in "normal times"—on the part of any government. In a very lucid text about the relationship existing between politics and reform in Latin America, Argentine sociologist Juan Carlos Torre indicated how a crisis that was collectively perceived opened up undreamed of government opportunities for new administrations. His analysis, developed on the basis of the Latin American experience, can be applied to the new American administration that took charge in January 2009. The Obama administration seemed to inaugurate a new government style with scarce prior commitments, and that also meant a generational change in the politics of the North. It is worthwhile to quote Torre extensively on the role of crisis in prompting policy changes:

> First of all, crises have the effect of discrediting the stances and ideas of the previous administration and this predisposes public opinion to grant those who attain power a strong mandate to act on the emergency. Second,

crises set up a sense of urgency that strengthens the belief that the lack of initiatives can only worsen matters; in these circumstances, scruples regarding which are the most appropriate procedures to make decisions give way to the acceptance of extraordinary decisions. Third, crises not only intensify collective problems but also generate a widespread fear of an increase in social conflicts and of threats to the institutional order. All of this broadens the margins of action of government leaders and intimidates the opposition forces. When these various mechanisms combine, a demand for governance is generated that allows the presidency to make full use of the necessary institutional resources to concentrate its decision-making authority, adopt policies elaborated in stealth by technocratic cabinets, and impose an expeditious procedure for their enactment.[3]

American Politics in Times of Hardship

How can we apply these reflections both to the internal and to the geopolitical situation of the US after the Bush era? First, we must determine whether the crisis is a partial, temporary, or random phenomenon, or if it is, instead, a steady and deep trend that requires extraordinary treatment. American opinion is divided with reference to this. During the 2008 presidential campaign two of the three finalists—the Republican John McCain and the Democrat Hillary Clinton—in spite of their differences had something in common: They were both seasoned politicians, skillful in the management of the government system as is. They counted on the support of powerful pressure groups whose conflicting interests would have inevitably led to the usual compromise and to "more of the same," that then would have been translated into quite weak policies, if not something worse—a political stalemate and reciprocal veto. Either of them, had they been elected, would have moved away from some of the especially unsuccessful policies of the Bush administration but nevertheless would have maintained others. They differed, however, in matters of taxation, judicial philosophy, and social philosophy at large. As to health insurance and social security the differences had more to do with degree than content. Perhaps the biggest difference between them was in tone, which replicated the traditional counterpoint between the two major parties before the G. W. Bush presidency. Candidate Barack Obama, on the other hand, was very different both in form and in content, though on the latter remained somewhat vague. This difference was the result of the generational change Obama represented. During the Democratic primaries, Obama became the spokesman of the youth, an electorate sector that had stood out for its absenteeism in all the presidential campaigns since the Vietnam War. Youth participation in the young candidate's campaign was astounding.[4] From a symbolic point of view, Obama represented the hope of a decisive change. From the color of his skin to his exotic name he was fundamentally a different character: he did not represent racial division but its supersession in the crossbreeding of ethnic groups and cultures that characterizes the new American society. As he often has said, he is a carrier of this synthesis in his very DNA. The new president is not a representative of the identity-based politics of the last 30 years but of a new syncretic identity. He is less of a conventional bipartisan and more of a unitarian.

According to Obama's declarations, that unity would be based on basic and necessary state policies for the whole country—beyond partisan differences. He has not described himself as a conservative or liberal in the American sense but as a modernizing reformer. Hence the link is between his image or style and the government task he intends to accomplish. The latter is based on updating the American economy and society in order to better adapt them to a dynamic and fractured world. His image—and the huge challenge it represents—is that of a new man for a new world. And even though important sectors of American society are ready for reformist leadership, the problem is that key American institutions are not. If this diagnosis is correct, a fundamental question must be raised: is American society as a whole willing to accept a change of cast and course? In other words, is there a crisis situation that is collectively perceived and capable of generating a demand for the government to adopt new, creative policies that are at the same time rational, that were until now either unimaginable or shelved due to the great established interests?

There are indications that the crisis is, in fact, perceived as serious by many sectors of the population and that, among them, there is a demand for "something new." In a democracy a simple majority, and sometimes only a plurality, is enough for a candidate, a program, or a party to prevail. In American history there are precedents that favor this last hypothesis. I am referring to the great economic and social crisis of the thirties. In his book about Franklin Delano Roosevelt, historian J. M. Burns describes how at the beginning of the New Deal, when Congress had to tackle the bank emergency law, the following happened: "Having been completed by the president and his advisors at two in the morning, the bill was still a draft. However, even during the scarce 45 minutes allotted to the debate in the premises voices claiming 'we need to vote…' were heard. The Chamber quickly approved the project by a show of hands; the Senate proceeded likewise a few hours later; the president enacted it with his signature at nine in the morning."[5] Compared to the thirties, the current Congress seems dysfunctional and stalled.

Meanwhile, there are signs that we have entered a period of converging crises and emergency situations. The most obvious are:

- a financial crisis
- an employment crisis

- a security crisis
- an environmental crisis
- an energy crisis
- an educational crisis
- a retirement and pension crisis
- a health insurance crisis
- a geopolitical crisis.

In the September 9/11 attack, and several years later with Hurricane Katrina, the American population has experienced grave disruptions. Social disruption is an experience that Latin Americans know well, and about which some of them have theorized.[6] Such incidents produce reactions of collective fear and a demand for safety and a "strong government." But there are other crises, more structural than interim in nature, that should generate a demand for a "rational government," that is, a willingness to support state policies in the fields of environment, energy, education, health, and foreign relations that exceed the conventional frame. These are positive demands—not punitive reactions—and require a stronger dose of hope than fear.

Deep down the great American choice is between fear and hope. Both feelings furnish a government with more freedom of action: one to punish and keep watch, the other to promote and dignify. From Latin America where people are used to granting great freedom of action to their governments that must face periodic and serious crises, one should hope that the long ongoing American crisis will produce, in the end, a healthy political reaction with unified support behind a new cast for different times. For a while, the new cast will have greater freedom of action. It is the opportunity every crisis provides to those in office in hard times. The greatest danger is that the rational reform may succumb to anxiety and to a punitive turn in politics.[7] The jury is still out.

The Return of Public Intervention

In the uncanny calm that followed the first wave of the crisis a new "systemic" rationality started making headway. Neither individuals nor single states, by themselves, are capable of engaging such rationality. Only international consensus and coordinated action can engage it. This is a novelty that will usher in a different geopolitical order in the years to come, if it does not fall apart due to the exigencies not of policy but of politics.

"By reason or by force" is the motto inscribed in the Chilean coat of arms. It dates back to 1812 and the Latin American wars of independence. Our own political correctness inclines us to reject it because it sounds bellicose and authoritarian. However, this iteration was not the original intent of the founding fathers of Latin American republics—self-made men who were guided by the principles of the European Enlightenment. For them, the goal of national independence was a just and rational objective. If it were not possible to attain it by negotiation, then military might would prevail.

The time of the wars of independence belonged to cultivated military men for whom reason and force went hand in hand. It was certainly the case of José de San Martín, the Argentine national hero, who was a member of the Philadelphia Lodge—a center of early North American enlightenment. Other cultivated generals were Bernardo de O'Higgins, the Chilean liberator, and Simón Bolívar—an officer far better educated than those who abuse his name today. Another Argentine general, Bartolomé Mitre, wrote a learned biography of a fellow military man (Manuel Belgrano) and also translated Dante's *La Divina Commedia* on the side while he was fighting wars. The Chilean motto is a version of the ancient Roman dictum *aut consiliis aut ense* (by counsel or by sword), which is at the origins of the concept of a state of law. The terms were elaborations by Romans of even older concepts in the philosophy of Plato, and have traveled through the centuries to reappear in any discussion of the relationship between knowledge and power (*consilium/auxilium*). Most Western representations of justice consist of a blindfolded woman holding a scale that balances Reason (a book of laws) and Force (a sword). One finds such images in seals and statues in most courts of justice today.

At the beginning of the administration of Chilean President Ricardo Lagos—exemplary in many ways—a debate took place in the Congress of that South American nation as to whether the motto "By reason or by force" should be kept (it brought back memories of the Pinochet era) or whether it should be exchanged for the less bellicose motto "By the force of reason." The discussion went nowhere and the decision was tabled for lack of a quorum. The result was for the better because the proposed change was a cowardly distortion of the original statement. And so the original forking judgment remained as sharp as ever: By reason or by force.

A Philosophical Dilemma

The forking judgment appears clearly in *The Republic* of Plato, who puts the words in the mouth of Socrates. The issue was none other than the relationship between the proper exercise of reason, on the one hand, and justice, on the other. The Greek philosophers observed quite sensibly that in everyday life, the common sense of people leads them to behave in many a devious manner—if and when they can get away with it. "Devious" would therefore seem to be "rational," when rational means convenient. Success is often the result of an expeditious use of less-than-proper means to attain an agreed-upon goal.

Those with fewer scruples often overtake those who are more punctilious, or plainly more honest. The calculus of individual gain trumps the spirit of solidarity. The norms of conviviality are often sacrificed in favor of competitive advantage. Even when they are obeyed, it is for fear of punishment or for mere convenience, and not by virtue of true conviction. As in the lyrics of the well-known tango *Cambalache*, the cheats have the advantage: "If one man lives by his forgeries and another steals his way to the top, it makes no difference if he's a priest, a mattress-dealer, the Ace of Clubs, a cutpurse or a cop!"

The ancient Greeks, thus, reached a disturbing conclusion: injustice can be a key to success. Faced with this apparent triumph of devious cleverness, Plato proposed (always through the medium of Socrates's reported statements) a superior argument. He effectively demonstrated that the very exercise of devious cleverness, that is, the unscrupulous use of reason for mere individual advantage is self-defeating in two basic ways: first, by undermining community; and second, by eventually turning like a boomerang on the practitioner.

In the first way, a "community" of elbowing advantage-seekers ends up canceling one and all initial individual advantage and ends up generating a general discomfort. Thus, let's say on a level field full of spectators at a soccer match, one person stands on tiptoe to see farther than her neighbor, then soon enough those around her will have to do the same thing; and in the end everybody will be standing in the same relative position to one another as before, except that everybody's feet will hurt. Individual cleverness ends up as collective silliness. In the second way, self-seeking behavior produces bad results over time because the improper use of resources for short-term advantage will lead to their depletion for those who follow us in life. We saddle our descendants with unsustainable burdens. Latin American history is full of examples of this syndrome: profligate todays and sorrowful tomorrows. They are the source of some of its best literature.[8] To put it differently, what is rational in a small context is irrational in a larger one. Or, reason is a function of scale. I don't know the mathematics of this statement, but I am sure those enamored of rational-choice models can figure it out.[9]

The Policy Dilemma

A market economy is subject to periodic fluctuations that are the cycles of boom and bust, growth and contraction. That rhythm is considered normal within certain parameters in a capitalist system. Nevertheless, in longer stretches of time a different set of crises—more severe and disruptive—erupt, such as the Great Depression of the thirties and the current Great Recession, or Third Depression, as it is sometimes called.[10] Both were the product of prior excess, wrong calls, and poor policies undertaken by authorities. The great critics of capitalism, from Marx to Kondratiev,[11] made reference to the difficulty—in a capitalist system—first, to anticipate and second, to prevent such big crises. The debacle is understood only after it starts. In other words, a rational understanding takes place retrospectively, when it is too late. Worse yet, the lessons of great crises are rapidly erased from the collective memory, especially after a recovery, thus sowing the seeds of future ones.

Sometimes the very crisis obliges the political leaders and the economic elite to take regulatory and control measures that, in due course, become institutionalized and which therefore delay a repetition of the syndrome for longer periods of time. But in the longer run the dynamics of the economy escapes the regulatory framework of the old institutions, bypasses their safeguards, and results in new crises—ever larger and more complex. Innovation—the essence of modern capitalism—has both a sunny side and a dark side. Only after the unexpected eruption of a novel crisis of great magnitude national states and international organizations are forced to engage in a new round of institutional innovation. Humanity moves forward looking resolutely to the past, stumbling upon hitherto unknown solutions to big problems—but only after trying a variety of solutions to past problems, like generals ready to fight the last war. Reason prevails belatedly, riding on the wings of force. As Hegel wrote, "the owl of Minerva takes flight when dusk is falling"—meaning that the understanding of a situation comes too late to do much about it.

The great crisis of the thirties forced the authorities of the wealthiest countries to establish programs of public works, pension systems, unemployment compensation schemes, control rules, and eventually international arrangements that lasted for decades and which postponed, if not averted, a repeat of economic disasters. After seven decades, the evolution of the global economy managed to overtake or bypass a number of these compensatory institutions, and once again the capitalist system careened out of control. Financial technologies and a new, more extensive and intensive pattern of globalization led, under those poorly regulated circumstances, to the current systemic crisis. Just as the decade of the Great Depression led to the Bretton Woods Agreement (a conference of powers held from 1–22 July 1944 to set up international financial institutions and a system of exchange rate management which remained in place until the early 1970s), the current crisis has already moved the steering of the world economy away from the conventional G-7 to the larger group of G-20, which includes the big emergent powers.

The net result is that the economic system acquires, by force, greater rationality. This increase of rationalization is neither the result of a dictatorial imposition from above—such as the enlightened despotism of eighteenth-century monarchs—nor the result of a revolutionary upheaval issuing in the "cult of reason" as during the French Revolution nor the "educational dictatorship" of the Bolsheviks at the beginning of last century. The main force today is the force of circumstance, leading whoever is in power to take measures of moderate rationality and state intervention. But even these measures, which may seem weak by the standards of previous eras, would have been inconceivable a few years ago, when an apparently endless bonanza made them seem utopian. The force today is what the French call *force majeure*— the forced passage from the micro to the macro-level, from the cry "every man for himself" to the cry "let's salvage the system."

What is the agency capable of carrying out, or at least steering, this shift? Systemic rationality is by definition beyond the scope and power of individual action—including the action of powerful but discrete groups. The only candidate, by default, is the state. But the state has changed as well (witness the Chilean debate about the motto, and the impasse it shows). It is no longer the nationalist state of yesteryear, although national states must, under the circumstances, reassume the role they had so often abdicated under neoliberalism; to wit: guarantee social order and internal peace, effect some measure of redistribution, reinforce a social safety net, and compensate and placate the losers in the big game that we call a crisis. When leaders are prone to act, it seems, is when there is a significant enough crisis that they are unable to avoid tough decisions. Every government—right, left, or center—has had to act during the financial emergency under the common rationality of *raison d'état*. Each one has instituted urgent policies of stabilization that we do not know how long or how deep they will reach. But the national state has become an investor of last resort, if not an owner of last resort. It has done so reluctantly, pushed by circumstance, or begged to do it by a private sector that by dint of privatizing so much collective value now feels the need to socialize its enormous losses. And so we are back at the beginning, under the motto of the Chilean coat of arms: *Por la razón o por la fuerza*.

There is another big difference this time. Decades of forced-draft globalization, which followed the opening up of hitherto out-of-bounds social systems, have transferred essential state functions to the international arena— without leading to global government. In the absence of the latter we must experiment with global *governance*; that is, the cooperation under duress of semi-sovereign nations. All the forces of globalization have rendered obsolete a return to narrower forms of state intervention. Stateness has replaced state, just as, in Michel Foucault's words, governmentality has replaced government. The state is not dead: it is superseded, sublated—in Hegel's terms *aufgehoben*. Herein lies a big challenge of our time.

In the thirties fully sovereign states rapidly descended into bad policies of "beggar thy neighbor" (protectionism and trade wars) until the tensions led to a massive military confrontation. Today any such move turns against the perpetrator almost immediately. Neither the tools nor the will are there, and that is an improvement over the past. Yet none of these arguments should lead us to complacency. There is no guarantee of success in a global risk society. The current recovery is not yet credible and bigger dangers lurk on the horizon. But this time "force" may lead to "reason" rather than to the collective folly of the past.

Braking the Fall

The sanitized language of political correctness notwithstanding, we have effectively entered the third Great Depression of the capitalist world.[12] I will offer an idea of the extent and the velocity of the decline in economic activity during the initial phase of the crisis and, above all, of the destruction of wealth around the world. It remains to be seen whether our governments' concerted action has managed to brake the fall. Likewise, the geopolitical consequences of this extraordinary collapse have yet to be fully experienced.

In the American vernacular when a business deal turns sour or an opportunity is lost one says, "it has gone South." With the ongoing destruction of wealth in the North, Latin Americans need to know what's coming down south. All figures are preliminary of course, as the crisis continues as of this writing.

During three years we have borne witness to an economic collapse that has no precedents, though lessons can be gleaned from the 1907 US banking crisis, the great financial/economic crisis of 1929–1932, and, more recently, the collapse of the world's second economy—Japan—in the 1990s.[13] This crisis is worse than all of those. In contrast to the Japanese crisis, this one is a synchronized, global crisis. And its magnitude is much greater than that of the Great Depression of 1929–1932. We are dealing with the possible collapse of the most recent phase of globalization. It is a reminder of the fact that until now the globalized economy has been effectively situated not just in the United States, but to be more precise, on Wall Street. And this financial center turns out to be the center of a donut: a hole.

It is a crisis that by virtue of its size and the specific dynamic of the capitalist system has swept across the world like a supernatural catastrophe, beyond any human control. In the face of this phenomenon, the planet's governments went to battle with all the fiscal and monetary tools at their disposal. The battle still rages. It is a pitched conflict: something out of science fiction, like *The War of the Worlds* (H.G. Wells, 1898) or the subsequent radio broadcast (Orson Wells, 1939) that the novel inspired. On one side, stands the sharpest economic contraction since 1980, the strongest deflationary wave since the Great Depression, the worst real estate collapse in history, and the highest tally of bankruptcies on record. To confront these demons, on the other side, stand our leaders who are ready with the largest combination of money issuance, government rescue packages, and stimulus plans ever tried.

The majority of politicians and economists hope that this defensive strategy succeeds in slowing and disarming the ghouls threatening the global system. They hope that governments can rescue nearly all of the great institutions that floundered and are still floundering; that they print money in order to correct retrospectively the many poor decisions made by big banks, insurance companies, and large manufacturers—who will then rebound from the current financial and credit paralysis (although without stopping to consider the causes); that they can maintain a high level of public debt (both foreign and domestic) for an indeterminate time; and that they will be able to counter deflation with inflation.

In the heat of the moment, however, they have not stopped to consider that, once unleashed, inflation will be very difficult to slow; that it may very well destroy the value of a currency; and that, in the long run, inflation can condemn capitalism to a painful fate. Others—whose ranks are thinnest but who are among the most orthodox thinkers—believe that this strategy (which was initiated in the final days of the Bush administration and was continued with fervor by the new Obama administration) may work in the short- and mid-runs, but that it may prove fatal in the long run. In their pessimistic view, the success of the strategy will be short-lived. They believe that, in spite of all their weapons, the intervening forces of government will fail to achieve their proposed objectives, namely:

– They will not succeed in reversing the long overdue liquidation of bad debts;
– They will not succeed in slowing the necessary decline in the cost and quality of life;
– They will not succeed in creating an inflationary exit strategy and lowering the value of the dollar;
– They will not succeed in delaying the days of hard work and sacrifice;
– They will not succeed in protecting inefficiency and discouraging innovation; and
– They will not succeed in institutionalizing mediocrity in the name of safety.

In the midst of the crisis, the lower house of the American Congress approved some $800 billion as a stimulus package. Meanwhile, the Treasury Department acknowledged the failure of its previous effort, the $700 billion troubled asset relief program (TARP) that was intended to inject money into the beleaguered financial sector. In the first skirmishes of this great battle, the great enemy—deflation – neutralized the best intervention plans.

Deflation is not merely a decline in prices, though right now this decline is plain to see. Deflation is something more: it represents an extreme case of wealth destruction. Of course, the further we explore the subject, the more doubts arise. Is the "artificially" generated product of reckless indebtedness rightfully called wealth? Many people, perhaps, would answer yes, since more goods and services are generated. But accountants, who tend to be more conservative in their assessments, would likely answer no, since the liabilities that sustain this wild generation of assets exceed the assets themselves and, from the accounting perspective, the net worth is negative. Could it be that wealth is simply a measure of assets, with the nature and size of liabilities wholly irrelevant (a formulation that lurks behind many of today's sector "bubbles")? Or, on the other hand, is wealth better conceived of as net worth? But, accounting itself has become an art of dissimulation—as revealed in the recent scandals regarding Greece's sovereign debt and the "cooking of the books."[14] Whatever the case may be, what is certain is that right now wealth is being destroyed at an accelerating pace and we are all feeling the impact in our daily lives. Compared to this destructive rhythm, governmental measures—for all their haste—are painfully slow. The most daring rescue packages are far smaller than the wealth being "burned" on a daily basis. And, more worrying still, our leaders have been unable to ensure that these funds reach those who truly need them. The wealth destroyed was several times larger than the most generous of the rescue packages. Each quarter, the US Federal Reserve publishes a detailed account of national wealth (fig.2) divided into five categories: real estate, corporate equities, mutual fund shares, pension and insurance reserves, and assets of non-profit non-governmental organizations, including universities, churches and foundations.

Figure 2: Wealth Destruction in the US 2007–2008. (Source: Federal Reserve, *Flow of Funds*)

Quarter	07 – 1	07 – 2	07 – 3	07 – 4	08 – 1	08 – 2	08 – 3
By sector:							
1 Real Estate	−53	−190	−496	−708	−662	−217	−647
2 Corporate	530	633	78	−377	−911	−247	−922
3 Mutual Funds	84	202	96	145	−297	−24	−523
4 Pensions	83	438	83	−265	−832	−132	−653
5 Non-profits	127	101	48	0	−32	−10	−128
Totals	782	1,184	−190	−1,495	−2,734	−630	−2,872

Total losses = $7,921 Billion.

The chart shows how in the first quarter of 2007 homes began to lose value in the real estate sector. This marked the beginning of the so-called sub-prime mortgage crisis, with losses totaling $53 billion. In the second quarter the losses ballooned to $190 billion. They increased in the third quarter ($496 billion) and rose again in the final quarter to $708 billion. It was in this quarter that wealth destruction spread to other sectors: stock market values, life insurance, pension funds. By the close of 2007 losses already totaled $1.5 trillion dollars (a trillion is a million millions, or 10 to the power of 12). This trend accelerated in 2008. Families lost about $3 trillion in real estate value in the first quarter and continued to lose in the second quarter, in spite of an economic stimulus package. In the third quarter, losses rose again to $3 trillion. By the end of the year, losses added up to nearly $8 trillion. The sum was eight times greater than the stimulus package proposed by Obama and eleven times greater than the Treasury's first rescue package (Secretary Paulsen's TARP program). Over the following several months, the government lavished new and sizeable sums on guarantee programs in order to prevent large institutions from going bankrupt. But money guaranteed was not the same as money spent. Institutions like Citibank teetered on the brink of bankruptcy, and there was talk of outright nationalization and/or liquidation of the banking giant.

For several decades, the US economy had borne increased levels of debt: mountains of loans, promissory notes, bonds, mortgages, credit cards, and bank paper accumulated year after year. But everything changed in the third quarter of 2007. It started with the liquidation of short-term debt in the interbank markets and in the corporate short-term debt market (commercial paper). Later, the liquidation extended to the mortgage sector and to bonds. In the third quarter of 2008, mass liquidation was already well underway (see Figs. 3 and 4).

Figure 3: Collapse of Mortgage Debt in the US. (Source: Federal Reserve, *Flow of Funds*. Table F4, Credit Market Borrowing)

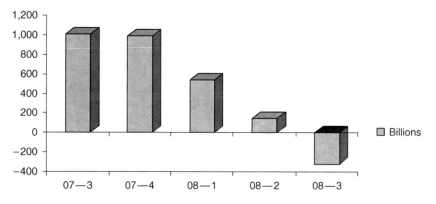

Figure 4: Acceleration of Wealth Destruction in the US 2007–2008. Losses in billions of dollars. (Source: Federal Reserve, *Flow of Funds*)

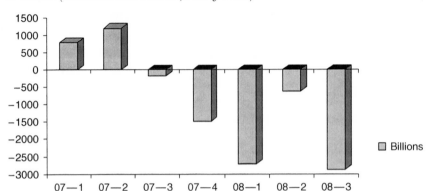

This all adds up to something much more serious than the exhaustion of credit, which is a decline in the creation of new debt. We are dealing with the destruction of unpaid debts that are then written off as losses. The process is plain to see in US towns and cities: fallen housing prices; mass mortgage foreclosure; and bankruptcy of creditor banks that have been forced to move their numbers from assets to liabilities. It is a classic, nearly textbook, cycle of deflation and debt collapse—strikingly similar to what happened between 1929 and 1932, though many would rather not admit it.

As if this were not enough, prices began to fall. In the early months of the crisis, the prices of commodities declined just as they did during the Great Depression. Oil fell 73 per cent, copper 66 per cent, nickel 73 per cent, platinum 66 per cent, and wheat 64 per cent, to give just a few examples. The Producer Price Index, which is more reliable and sensitive than the Consumer Price Index, dropped at a rate of 2 per cent per month. Naturally, all of this was reflected in the Dow Jones Industrial Average, which suffered the worst plunge in its 75-year history.

In the face of such debacle, government-spending programs have been inadequate. As cowboys like to say, you can lead a horse to water, but you can't make it drink. The massive sums of money lent to the banks did not leave the vaults. Whom were the banks going to lend to? Meanwhile, manufacturers announced massive layoffs and shelved plans for new investment and construction. They simply had too much idle capacity. It is fitting to remember what Marx had maintained: The roots of capitalist crises lie not in too few goods but too many. There are too many unsold houses, too clothes waiting to be bought, too many unused offices, and too many empty shopping malls.

The Obama administration initiated a series of public works projects, similar in form but not in size to Franklin Roosevelt's WPA in 1933. It was easier said than done. The risk of such measures is that, executed too hastily, they merely multiply useless programs. Even then, the programs seemed to be too small and come too late. But, without quick action, the economy would simply continue its precipitous decline. This was the dilemma that Obama inherited: to boldly try to reverse the course, or just settle for putting on the brakes? A historical warning was readily available: In the nineties Japan executed a stimulus package consisting of an outlay of 10.7 trillion yen in August 1992, 13.2 trillion yen in April 1993, 6.2 trillion yen in September 1993, 15.3 trillion yen in February 1994, 14.2 trillion yen in September 1995, 16.7 trillion yen in April 1998, 23.9 trillion yen in November 1998, and 18 trillion yen in November 1999. The total was 118.2 trillion yen, equivalent to $1.3 trillion in today's dollars (adjusted for inflation and GDP relative to the US economy). All this amounted to nothing: Japan lost a decade mired in mediocre or no growth and falling stock prices. Did Roosevelt's stimulus and public works package fare any better in the 1930s? Studies on the subject— among them one by Ben Bernanke, chairman of the US Federal Reserve—are far from conclusive. And the debate continues over why, with all of Roosevelt's stimulus packages, it was not until 1943—in the middle of the Second World War—that the US economy finally recovered.

Will we have better luck, or will we have to endure ten years of economic stasis and social tensions followed by more wars? This is the big question that looms over the hitherto strongest economy in the world.

The Day After

What did the principal countries gain with the various rescue measures they adopted in face of the financial crisis? They gained time. But gaining time is not a strategy. At best it is a tactic that may be used to engage real reforms—to set in place regulatory structures, to mitigate global inequality, to reorganize societies around a more austere lifestyle, to energize the bottom of the social pyramid, and to establish the bases for new patterns of sustainable development. At worst, however, additional time merely postpones the day of reckoning.

In the third quarter of 2009, the American GDP was said to have grown by 3.5 per cent from the bottom of the hole in which the economy had fallen during the previous year's financial meltdown. Armed with that figure, most mainstream economists—the same economists that missed the crisis two years ago—declared, "The crisis is over."[15] The headlines in the press conveyed a sense of renewed confidence, albeit still cautious, that the day after things are not as bad as they had feared.

The measures taken by the government of the United States and by the governments of all industrial nations—Europe, Japan, and some of the

BRICs—prevented a veritable catastrophe, the kind of social and political disaster that followed the "crack" of 1929–30.[16] This time there was rapid and coordinated action on the part of most countries, or at least by the G-20. They all launched anti-cyclical programs by injecting large amounts of cash into the stalled banking sector. Moreover, they committed to not beggaring their neighbors—that is, to not engage in protectionist practices like the competitive devaluation of their currencies.

Governments took hold of accumulated public savings to rescue financial institutions deemed "too big to fail." By and large, governments did not nationalize the banks. Instead they socialized their losses. Public funds from taxpayers were also used to bail out the dysfunctional automotive enterprises that were once the pride of American industry, and to bail out the largest private insurers which, together with the banks, had triggered the crisis by assuming unsustainable risks through opaque financial instruments like the now infamous credit default swaps (CDS).[17] In other words, governments organized a sort of slow-motion bankruptcy restructuring of big players at the top of the social pyramid. Nevertheless, the rescue program had worrisome characteristics, some of which may herald the onset of an even bigger future crisis. There are several reasons for such concern.

First, the rescue was undertaken by individuals and cliques directly and indirectly linked to the very same institutions whose crackpot behavior triggered the crisis in the first place. There already exists an entire library of studies—some good, some bad, most middling—which describe the emergency measures and how they were taken.[18] Popular culture has an expression that may portray the situation: "putting the fox in charge of the chicken coop." In the early scramble of *sauve qui peut* (every man for himself) the powerful financial clans came out ahead.

Second, the result has been an even greater concentration of finance capital at the top, and the consolidation of its steering position in the global economy on the whole and in the hole. The reality of late capitalism approaches a caricature, and the caricature seems to follow the script of bygone Marxists like Rudolf Hilferding and V.I. Lenin.[19] Like all processes of economic concentration, this one, too, involved a degree of cannibalism at the top. An emblematic example was the fall of the house of Lehman Brothers to the ultimate benefit of the competition (J. P. Morgan, Goldman Sachs, and even Citibank). It was a blood sacrifice—what Thorstein Veblen called an atavistic remnant of barbarian times among the economic elites. As one of the big players was served on the altar of the crisis, the ensuing panic about a generalized collapse (or in the sanitized lingo of policy makers, a "systemic risk") provoked a frantic scramble of rescue measures to save the remaining financial clans. Had Lehman been rescued, the public reluctance to follow suit with the others (leading most likely to a Congressional veto on bailouts) would have led to their serial demise, like a stream of falling dominos. It would have resulted in a total paralysis of banking, and in a forced banking holiday like the one F. D. Roosevelt decreed when 75 years ago the entire economy went bankrupt and unemployment reached 25 per cent of the labor force. As befits an earlier era of greater stamina and courage, conditions were decidedly more dire and remedies much stronger then than illness suffered and the medicine purveyed by the Obama administration today. So far, no Rooseveltian *grand coup d'autorité* has taken place, and as a consequence the same cast of financial characters do what they have always done: reap mega-profits, resist and evade regulation, move one step ahead of the controlling authorities, and continue to inhabit the old world of predation and chicanery. In Wall Street they are conscious of the fact, and plume themselves a little with it. They have no problem in acknowledging their tricks with smug candor when interviewed by sociologists.

Third, the surviving financial clans captured the public funds released to reboot the economy and restarted trading again in their magic world of self-referentiality, using financial instruments as opaque as those that led to the crisis. The funds have not found their way to the productive economy at home, they have not eased the pain of unemployment, and they have not stemmed the wave of destitution at the bottom of the social pyramid. Instead they have led speculating in commodities soft and hard, playing games of carry trade,[20] borrowing at negative interest rates at home and profiting from juicy interest rates abroad, and creating along the way new asset bubbles in emerging markets. These new asset bubbles in the wider globe (*orbi*) have replaced the punctured asset bubble at home (*urbi*). The economic revival, although it generates handsome profits for some, seems once more based on "fictitious capital," which is what sustains a modest level of economic activity and a semblance of recovery. Under these circumstances, it is difficult to distinguish a bounce in the stock market from a dead cat's bounce in the real world. Some countries like Brazil have felt compelled to impose a tax on the inflow of speculative funds, and many emerging economies are worried about the upward trend of their currencies. In short, public stimulus funding has produced so far concentrated financial profits and a lot of speculative action in the markets.

Fourth, there is no visible easing of credit from the financial sector to either the productive world of real small and medium enterprises, or the consumer and housing sectors. Thus, the recovery is shabby both at the quantitative and the qualitative levels. For the United States, there is a renewal of exports, due in large part to the debasement of the currency (an inevitable consequence of massive debt and public stimulus through the printing press). But it is hard to imagine that the world's largest debtor and the world's largest consumer market can go back on track pulled by the locomotive of exports.

Fifth, the most dramatic index of continuity and even aggravation of the crisis in the real economy is the relentless climb of unemployment and the retrenchment of consumption. For many years ahead, the American population will have to adjust to a lower standard of living, or to put it more elegantly, to a way of life leaner than that to which they have grown accustomed.

Sixth, the sociological corollary of the present process of sham recovery is an increase of inequality at both the national and the international levels. Such social regression is more visible in some advanced countries like the United States than in others like Germany, and in some developing countries like Argentina than in others like Brazil. The effect is directly related to the quality of public policies of redistribution and the design of state intervention, the star examples being in this respect and with all critiques of the model notwithstanding the Scandinavian countries.[21] Here public intervention in health, education, and pensions is key. In the emerging world there are cases like China where increasing inequality has been mitigated by the overall rise in prosperity and by the birth of new middle classes. But we must not forget that the present recovery is a checkered process, and that the crisis has left a sequel of destitution, hunger, and malnutrition at the bottom of world society. The United Nations has estimated that there are 1.02 billion human beings who are hungry and that the number is rising. As Argentine economist Roberto Mizrahi maintains in his latest book *International Crisis: Adjusting the Course and Improving the Systemic Functioning*,[22] inequality is the silent and deep cause of the crisis. In this respect, a recovery that increases rather than decreases inequality is not sustainable. We should harbor no illusions about the self-healing propensity of the present economic arrangements.

Seventh, as mentioned before, we are living through the aftermath of one punctured bubble but we are not immune from larger and worse bubbles, some of them a consequence of the rescue policies themselves. While there is a severe dearth of funds in the real economy, there is a glut of speculative funds in the financial orbit, ready to pump up different assets the world over. Whereas the bursting of the last bubble in real estate provoked a crisis that spread from the center to the periphery of the world economic system, the next bubbles may burst here and there, sequentially or simultaneously in various corners of that system. Speculative funds are flocking to hard commodities like gold, energy, and minerals, or to soft commodities like water and foodstuffs, to the bonds and stocks of emerging markets, or to fun and games with currency trades. The danger therefore is that the next crisis may be a devastating metastasis.

In sum, we are witnessing a timid, sputtering recovery, largely sustained by public intervention, or by the wanton throwing of money at each and every problem in the short run. But these policies will sooner rather than later run out of strength, especially in light of a looming fiscal crisis for each and every government at the central and at the local level. When we reach that point, governments will face the dwindling of their resources, a mountain of debt to service, and a very tight spot to maneuver. The failure to manage deftly these crisscrossing pressures may well place "serious" economies in the same predicament that Latin American countries faced in the past.[23] They may be caught in the vise of debt and forced to ride the roller coaster of deflation/inflation, social stress, and political instability. Welcome to the world of future first-world pesos. The specter of depression has not been exorcized.

The Day After the Day After

What have the leading economies gained through the various rescue packages launched in parallel and in coordination? On the positive side, they have gained a bit of time to design new structures of world economic growth, which are: better (by which I mean enabling) regulation, lesser inequality, greater austerity, less waste, cleaner energy, and a spark of entrepreneurial hope at the bottom of the social pyramid.

In the past three decades the world has gone through, despite all problems, a marvelous revolution in information technologies. The next marvelous revolutions will be in the bio-medical and energy sectors. Health, R&D, and energy are the bright spots of the future. Greed, predation, and gambling are its dark spots. If growth is to be sustainable it must be global and fair. It is becoming increasingly clear that the alternative is the Hobbesian universe of "warre of all against all." Therefore, it is worthwhile reviewing the fundamental premise for sustainability.

There must be a convergence in the quality of life of the present "underdeveloped" and "overdeveloped" worlds. The point of convergence is that delicate spot in a double escalator in which the ascending and the descending crowds detain their motion and choose a new and joint point of departure. To continue along the present pathways will lead to endless nasty troubles. There is a growing awareness of the problem and a serious thinking of the issues, and not just in the ivory towers of the developed world. For instance, the Chinese authorities and a number of Chinese intellectuals know full well that current rescue policies, such as large investment in infrastructure, aid to export companies, and calibration of the currency, useful as they may be in the short run, are not long-range solutions.[24] The longer view requires a re-orientation of economic activities to satisfy the pent-up demand of the domestic market, but in a manner that does not repeat the excesses and distortions of the overdeveloped world. They are figuring out growth scenarios based on greater equality, and a uniform standard of living, which they call "tempered well-being." They also envisage a rebalancing of world trade in a South-South direction. That is going beyond rescue tactics. It is strategic thinking.

In the context of the "day after" the current crisis, China occupies a geopolitical key place. No wonder then, that strategic initiatives, not well understood by the West, are taking place in the "middle kingdom." These initiatives are for the day after the day after. Anna Maria Jaguaribe, a Brazilian sociologist who has spent several years in China, has recently reported on Chinese strategic initiatives in the field of alternative development.[25] Her report lays out the terms of the ongoing debate in Chinese policy and intellectual circles. Of particular significance is the concept of "tempered welfare or well-being" (*xiao kang she hui*). It refers to a strategy of development that is not bent on the Western idea of "trickle down" prosperity, but of a more egalitarian "bottom up" capitalist economic growth, which blends the full spectrum of urban and rural life, and has surprising similarities to the successful model of regional development centers that has taken root in Northern Italy. Not only are these dynamic centers of innovation and profits, but they also have a limited "carbon footprint," are "environmentally friendly" and, given the scale, more accountable to local populations. Green, sustainable, and intelligent are the hallmarks of these experiments.[26]

Just as ascending China seeks to temper growth or channel it in sustainable pathways, so the advanced world of late capitalism in Europe and the US will have to learn to live well with less. Just as there are creative ways to manage "emergence" so there are creative and humane ways to manage "decadence." It is not an easy geopolitical task, and there are few past examples of non-bellicose rebalance. For the United States this is an uphill political and intellectual task in a downhill economic environment. It means shedding not only the obsolete business models of the past but also the obsolete ideological models of unequal growth, and the over-dependence on outmoded forms of – to cite only three – conspicuous consumption, transportation, and security. Above all, it means shedding the fetishistic protection of high finance—a social sector that is predatory and over-concentrated—and whose social utility is largely unwarranted. Much has been written in derogatory tones about the new class of Russian "oligarchs." It is time to examine with the same critical eye the parasitic world of the American financial oligarchs—in the name of that old principle of democracy in America, whose attraction has remained intact from the days of Tocqueville to our own.

Chapter Four

A PAUCITY OF THOUGHT
AND ACTION

The Need for Different Paradigms

The global crisis is also an intellectual provocation, and the discipline of economics has not risen to the challenge. Why not? The problem lies perhaps in its search for a universal model that is unattainable, and in a subsequent flight from empirical reality. To get our feet back on the ground, we need to rethink the assumptions behind economic modeling and also rethink the institutional organization of research and higher education.

"Wanted: A new Galileo or Copernicus capable of reformulating economic theory. Please present models to the top twenty economics departments in the world (according to the *US News and World Report* rankings). If you fail to receive any replies, proceed to the top twenty sociology departments." Imagine this ad in an internationally recognized newspaper like *Le Monde, Corriere Della Sera, Financial Times*, or *The Wall Street Journal*.

Today's world leaders are struggling in vain to shed some light on the economic gloom brought about by the global crisis. Their tool of choice: the dim lantern of a low-amperage Keynesianism. I imagine that they are asking themselves: How can I be the next Franklin Delano Roosevelt? It seems that they are not finding any answers.[1]

The last few years have not been kind to the reputation of economists. For more than two decades, we watched as the profession rose in prestige. Today, however, economists are blamed for failing to note the fundamental fragility of the financial markets and for not anticipating the ensuing crisis. And with the global economy in ruin, these same economists are unable to agree on policy or on the probable course that the crisis will run.

In the previous chapter I pointed out the diverse "schools" of economic rescue packages put forth by both mainstream economists and those on the periphery. Each package is distinct, but all of them share two characteristics: They are vague, and they are intellectually mediocre.

Ironically, more economic research has been conducted during the last quarter century than during all of history. Nonetheless, in the midst of this crisis, the most cited economists are the dead ones: John Maynard Keynes, Irving Fisher, and Hyman Minsky, for instance.[2] All of these men belong to past generations.[3]

Since the 1960s economists have been engaged in a grand pursuit to establish the microeconomic foundations of macroeconomics. The guiding premise is that policy decisions, such as those affecting growth and inflation, boom and recession, ought to be based on the study of individual behavior. These economists have worked to build models based on the rational behavior of individuals who seek to "optimize" their interests. But this "ideal type" (*homo oeconomicus*) represents a stylization of a cultural-historic configuration that does not exist except perhaps as an approximation in one global corner of capitalism[4] and that fails to adequately explain both individual and social behavior even in those places where it is culturally legitimate.

In general, however, economists have embraced this paradigm and believe that their collective efforts have been a success. In leading US universities and, indeed, throughout the globalized world, the discipline of economics far outstrips the other social sciences in terms of resources, prestige, and compensation. Economists occupy a privileged position in the academic hierarchy.[5]

Yet, it is worth noting that in today's research universities, laurels are auto-referential— which makes it difficult to gauge their real worth. Researchers within each field determine who among their peers will be rewarded for their academic performance. This is the primary obstacle to interdisciplinary research by problem area, as opposed to the prevailing model, intradisciplinary research by specialization. In the social sciences, the highest praise goes to those who apply the most rigorous (read "mathematical") methodology. And the economists take the cake in this respect. Positioned thus at the pinnacle of the university hierarchy, whose highest level is membership in the coveted Nobel Prize club, economists have effectively barricaded themselves behind a wall of ego and self-inflation. The ivory tower has never seemed so opaque and remote.

There is no denying, of course, that economics is precise and that it is elegant. But formal elegance has little to do with the empirical reality. Those who have to establish and implement public policy and those who have to make concrete decisions for small, mid-size, and large businesses, along with the salesmen, workers, and general public, have little use for these models, despite their formal attractiveness. What people really want to know is how these models can be applied to advance their interests and, in turn, contribute to national prosperity. They want explanations that illuminate rather than obfuscate. Sadly, they don't get them. There is an economic science, but only a limited economic imagination.[6]

At times the self-referential arrogance seems excessive. One Nobel Prize winner, professor Robert Lucas—who was recognized for grounding macroeconomics in microeconomics—went so far as to put forth a thesis, known among his peers as the "Lucas critique," that argued that economic predictions should not be subject to normal statistical confirmation because such test would jeopardize the parsimony of models. The attitude brings back an apocryphal anecdote about the great German idealist, Georg Wilhelm Friedrich Hegel. After a conference, Hegel was cornered by a critic who insisted that the philosopher's theories did not accord with the facts. "Too bad for the facts," was Hegel's response (*Umso schlimmer für die Tatsachen!*).

The problem seems to lie in the search for a universal model of behavior based on facile premises. Economics, unlike physics, is not a hard science. Physicists have been searching for a "theory of everything" for quite some time. Einstein failed trying: For him, the "theory of everything" involved reducing the universe into fundamental particles located in a unified field. But, what in physics is an unattained but possible goal, in economics becomes a quixotic adventure: something like the encyclopedic ambitions of Bouvard and Pecuchet, Flaubert's endearing fools. The search for a single theory of everything at the deep ontological level of complex human behavior is foolhardy.

Based on simplistic premises, economists have reached complex conclusions. The same thing happened five centuries ago in the context of Ptolemy's theory (which, in fact, originated in the sixth century BC). Accepted as dogma by the medieval Church, this theory held that the Earth was the center of the universe. It adequately explained the apparent movement of the stars, the sun, and the planets. And even today Ptolemy's model provides a sound basis for navigating on the open sea using a sextant, a watch, astronomical charts, and a bit of spherical trigonometry. The model enables making precise calculations about particular circumstances despite its underlying flaws. Since the earth is not the center of the solar system, however, the Ptolemaic system is unable to explain the anomalies that appear in other calculations. To address these, Ptolemy's followers formulated numerous ad hoc explanations, which incorporated the idea of "epicycles." In the end, a set of complex, baroque explanations was needed to justify Ptolemy's estimates. Galileo and Copernicus revolutionized astronomy by changing the underlying premise and shifting the reality. Since that time, we have known that our planet revolves around the sun, though this might not appear to be so when the sun rises and sets. Today, with the global crisis raging, things are not obeying the existing economic models. And economists are hastily adding cycles and epicycles. What we need is a new Galileo or Copernicus in political economy.

The idea that economics can provide a general theory of human behavior rests on two fundamental assumptions: the pure rationality of actors and the efficiency of markets. But these assumptions are themselves irrational in their persistent denial of inconvenient facts. Valid theories have a more modest scope and are based on the formation and evolution of beliefs and the advancement of empirical knowledge about behavioral patterns. This is the way things work in the other social sciences, which have generally been dismissed by economists precisely because they do not offer general theories that are sufficiently general and tight. Efforts by sociologists, for instance, to formulate a general theory were abandoned after the 1950s, and this paved the way for the advancement of that discipline as a whole.

And yet, there remains an important holdout of purists who really believe that their models can explain all of human behavior and that realities like values and norms that do not fit in any rational scheme and all those elements that, loosely speaking, constitute culture are baseless and imprecise speculations—no different than fairy tales. This hardcore view borders on zealotry.

For those whose focus is the real world, these dogmatic theories are much too rigid. The premises of rational action and the efficiency of markets are simple to understand. The problem is that they are fictions. Many of the dilemmas confronting economists today—such as profit generation and the instability of global markets—can be traced to the failure of their existing models in concrete situations. Stock crashes, the incorrect valuation of assets, and the lack of information among actors have brought us to where we are today, and economists have little to say on such themes.

Findings from all the social sciences—including economics—are always approximate and provisional. The most useful economics theories are those that consist of mid-range hypotheses and shed light on particular situations.[7] The best course is to base research on empirical regularities, incorporate advanced statistics, and embrace the "grammar" of norms and values that guide behavior. This in itself is no small task. Still, the results from this kind of research are more useful than the search for more ambitious, general theories. The social sciences are part of the same epistemological class as engineering and medicine: They are diagnostic tools that facilitate public and private action. They are pragmatic—not paradigmatic—disciplines.

The global crisis is at once a disaster and an invitation to think differently. It is also a crisis in the way we organize knowledge. And since most research today is conducted in universities, it may be time to rethink the university itself, with an eye toward dismantling existing academic divisions and reassembling them into interdisciplinary teams focused on practical challenges and complex problems. We have tried the path of isolation among the different disciplines and a kind of super-specialization within them. The time has come for inclusive teams comprised of experts from diverse fields laboring on common tasks.[8]

Leadership in Question

A global crisis that began in the center would require strong leadership, also starting in the center. So far, such leadership has been either lacking, or hesitant, or blocked. In the countries of the global South, and in Latin America in particular, there has been sporadic posturing on the part of some leaders, and the silent hope among the others that things will sort themselves out, but there have been no clear exit strategies and no rational proposals. During the Great Depression there was much stronger leadership and more original theorists. Nonetheless it took thirteen years and a world war for the crisis to be sorted out. Finally, after Bretton Woods a global economy emerged, centered in the United States.[9] Today there is greater integration and greater coordination, and also less bellicosity, but there is no decisive leadership and only a very limited imagination.

A major victim of the global crisis has been the credibility of the US-based global capitalist system. One surprising consequence of the economic turmoil, apart from independent and joint efforts by leading countries to brake the plunge into a depression, has been the exposure of the dangerous, uncontrolled proliferation of financial capital in the very center of the system. Recent studies on the economy have reached similar diagnoses and unexpected analogies about this situation.[10]

At the height of the crisis and the ensuing panic, in the group photo taken at the closing of the 2009 meeting of the twenty leading industrialized and emerging nations in London, the leaders of the world radiated "official satisfaction" on stage. They put on a good face in bad times. They put away their differences and agreed on three sets of coordinated measures: one, the use of funds to stimulate demand and trade; two, improved vigilance of the financial and parallel financial sectors; and three, the elimination of "fiscal paradises." Perhaps the most impressive outcome of this summit was the announced revamping and recapitalization of the International Monetary Fund for the purpose of providing a life raft for those countries that were barely staying afloat, no doubt anticipating sovereign debt crises in the future. None of these measures, however, addressed the root of the crisis, the bottomless pit of destroyed value and ways to make these sums disappear from accounting ledgers. While the new measures did put forth a new financial architecture with the aim of avoiding future economic train wrecks, they failed to take stock of the real dimensions of the crisis. The measures were structural only in part. Meanwhile, production, international trade, and employment continued in free-fall. Nonetheless, at every subsequent summit all agreed that more was achieved than they had originally expected.

Considering that Latin Americans are used to viewing the US as a hegemonic ogre—benevolent or sinister, depending on their political ideology—recent opinions published by distinguished American economists (conservative and liberal) on the economic crisis caught Latin Americans by surprise. These opinions compared the American crisis (and, by extension, the global crisis) to the crisis in the so-called emerging markets over the last ten years, particularly the disasters in Argentina and Russia at the turn of this century. Until recently, it would not have occurred to anyone in the first world that a process of financial and economic disintegration that took place in Argentina between 2001 and 2002, or that a Russian-style default like the one in 1998, could happen in the world's leading power.[11]

Simon Johnson, a professor at MIT, was until recently the lead economist at the International Monetary Fund. In a recent issue of *The Atlantic*, he published a very interesting essay[12] in which he said that the current American crisis reminded him of the crises that he had to deal with ten years before in Argentina, Russia, and Malaysia. "In each of those cases, global investors, afraid that the country or its financial sector wouldn't be able to pay off mountainous debt, suddenly stopped lending . . . This is precisely what drove Lehman Brothers into bankruptcy on September 15 . . ." Johnson wrote. The "masters of the universe," owners of the financial kingdom of Wall Street behaved like Russian oligarchs, Johnson maintained.[13] They speculated recklessly, took on enormous risks with other peoples' money (above all, the savings of pensioners, who did not have the least idea that someone was playing roulette with their money) and took comfort in the likelihood that the government would run to their rescue if their bets failed.

Far away and long ago, in Argentina (an emerging market at the time, Argentina enjoyed the second highest per capita income in the world) a similar situation was described in detail in Julian Martel's novel *La Bolsa* (The Stock Market), whose context was the financial panic of 1890.[14] Fifteen years later in the US, Louis D. Brandeis—a commercial lawyer and future member of the Supreme Court—warned the public of the combined risk of greed, lack of transparency and limited vigilance in the financial sector in his book titled *Other Peoples' Money—and How the Bankers Use It*.[15] The years and economic cycles went by, bringing the 1907 Banker's Panic, which compelled J. P. Morgan to "cleanse" the financial sector of crooks and clowns, and the "First" Great Depression of the 1930s. In response to that event, the US Senate put Wall Street's leading bankers on the witness stand. The revelations were sensational. The practices uncovered were as absurd as they were obscene. The Senate commission's lead investigator, whose job was to interrogate the bankers, was Ferdinand Pecora. Years later, in 1939, Pecora published his notes and memories in the book *Wall Street under Oath*.[16] His work underscores how little we have learned in the subsequent 80 years of capitalist evolution.

I obtained a copy of Pecora's book from New York University's library. No one had checked it out in years. Reading its pages was like sitting in on a modern-day hearing of a Congressional investigation committee. The characters were nearly the same; the excesses and errors made were exceedingly similar. The only significant difference was the interplay between four factors: the volume of funds, the velocity of their movement, global reach, and the mathematical formulas employed in speculation.[17] Those examples suggest similarities between the crises of capitalism then and now.

Today, critics are going a step further, drawing comparisons between the financial sectors in the US and in emerging markets. Perhaps these resonances are an undesired side effect of the intense wave of globalization that began in 1989.

Johnson did not mince words in his *Atlantic* magazine article. He even broached a taboo topic: the potential of the US becoming a banana republic. And Johnson was not the only one applying the derogatory label. Another leading liberal economist, the Nobel Prize winner Paul Krugman, used the phrase as well.[18] The term also resonated with still another Nobel Prize-winning economist, Joseph Stiglitz.[19] Both Krugman and Stiglitz had studied the Argentine crisis of 2001–2002 in detail. Neither are analysts to be taken lightly. In defense of Argentina, I can only say that it does not grow bananas. They are imported from Brazil.

But it is not only liberal economists who respect Johnson, economists of other persuasions—like Larry Summers, who is president Obama's trusted economic advisor and hardly a liberal enthusiast—concur with Johnson's criticisms. Interestingly, Johnson's assessment coincided with those from Desmond Lachman, another ex-director of the IMF, who was formerly a Wall Street banker and is today an economic analyst for the ultra-conservative American Enterprise Institute. Statements from the conservative Lachman seem to echo the liberal views of Johnson.[20] Lachman explained that, when he traveled to countries with troubled, emerging economies in his former role with the IMF, he felt like a fortunate man. "At the time, I could not imagine that anything remotely similar could happen in the United States. . . . These days, though, I'm hardly so confident. Many economists and analysts are worrying that the United States might go the way of Japan, which suffered a 'lost decade.' . . . I'm more concerned that the United States is coming to resemble Argentina, Russia and other so-called emerging markets . . ."

To explore the matter further, I set out in search of studies with a broader, more sociological perspective, looking particularly for research from outside the US in order to counterbalance single influences. Standing out among these studies, by virtue of its depth and objectivity, was one conducted recently by Ronald Dore, an expert on the Japanese economy, who is currently conducting research on the financialization of the global economy at the London School of Economics.[21]

Dore's thesis is as follows. The instability of the global economic system, which has been plain to see over the last decade, is a consequence of a growing dominance of financial capital over the real economy. Dore presents a detailed study of the origins and the advance of the financialization of the economy. According to this author, it is not merely a matter of the increasingly mortgaged, complex, and incomprehensible character of the forms of mediation between those with savings and those in the real economy who need credit and insurance. The dominance of financial capital, says Dore, can also be traced to the nearly universally accepted principle that the sole purpose of a business is to maximize profit for its shareholders.

This belief, in turn, sustains the idea that the primary function of government is the creation and maintenance of a "shareholder culture." The doctrine has its roots in the Chicago School and in the preaching of the brilliant monetarist Milton Friedman, the father of modern neoliberalism. Dore's thesis is thus deeply sociological, as it attributes the financialization of the economy to a process of massive ideological indoctrination and the resulting culture. The social consequences of this hegemony are, for the author, negative. Among these consequences, he cites an increase in inequality both within and between societies, growing personal insecurity (as related to health, aging, and education), a brain drain toward the most speculative sectors of the economy and the erosion of mutual confidence and of feelings of solidarity. All of this contributes to uncontrolled economic growth, culminating in systemic crises of massive proportions.

These diagnoses distance critics on both the right and left from the Obama administration and its strategy to address the crisis. The Obama strategy consists of recapitalizing the financial sector with a massive injection of taxpayer funds while leaving infected structures in place and helping to purge toxic assets. Critics (from both sides) are skeptical about that approach. They compare the strategy to moving new furniture into a burning building. They are in favor, instead, of more drastic measures for the financial sector: state surgery or natural death.

Left-leaning liberals support the outright nationalization of big banks on the verge of bankruptcy, restructuring them, selling or eliminating toxic assets, and then privatizing the financial sector in a more manageable, structured incarnation. In short, they want to impose state discipline (an approach similar to the one used by the Swedish government in response to the 1990 Scandinavian bank crisis). For Johnson—the most Jacobin of the critics—the way forward embraces the very decapitation of the financial oligarchy. Dore, on the other hand, seems to favor a cultural revolution. The pure conservatives, meanwhile, advocate a different solution altogether: market discipline. In other words, they believe that the market's own functioning will ultimately eliminate bad sectors, and that no state-sponsored first-aid is required. They have faith in the flexibility, productivity, and creative energy of American society. This was the tactic used by President Hoover before he lost power to Franklin Delano Roosevelt in 1932. And, in fact, "Hooverism" has enjoyed a kind of resurrection among conservatives and market fundamentalists. This camp has adopted a revisionist view of the New Deal, one that critiques Roosevelt's methods of leading the country out of economic crisis. Today, as in the past, they fail to consider the political cost of an economic free fall.

We are therefore at a crossroads where three paths diverge, what the Romans called a *trivium*. The government has opted for the middle road. But the choice is hardly trivial. In fact, the middle road might be the riskiest of the three.

Chapter Five

THE NEW WORLD IN A CHANGED WORLD

Pictures, it is often said, are worth a thousand words. For sociologists, figures and tables can have a similar eloquence. In the simple projections below (Figure 5), the figures of the International Monetary Fund tell the story of a post-crisis "recovery" that entails a geo-political realignment in the concert of nations, and provide substance to the expression "emerging markets."

In the first chapter of this book I tried to present the main contours of a new global division of labor that combined the Chinese and the American economies. Chinese exports and American consumption led the world's economic growth. From 2000 on, this symbiosis produced robust rates of growth in the American economy and spectacular rates of growth for the Chinese. At the time and on the surface, it seemed like a "win-win" arrangement. As one took a closer look, however, one noticed something strange and lopsided about such grand deal. As early as 2005, and to an observer not blinded by the irrational exuberance of the markets, the bargain did not seem sustainable for too long. It was beset by a peculiar imbalance. In essence, the bargain consisted of a credit line from the People's Republic to the United States that allowed Americans to overspend, that is, to live beyond their means—an indulgence that American policy makers had always scolded Latin Americans for practicing with irresponsible abandon.

For many years the control of overspending was the essence of IMF recipes of stabilization for developing countries, under unchallenged American influence. That often resulted in pro-cyclical policies that threw many a country into a ditch. The experience showed that sometimes "doing the prudent thing" was foolish, and confirmed the barb of William Blake, which would be an apt epitaph for the old IMF: "Prudence is a rich ugly old maid, courted by Incapacity."

We have come a long way. The Latin American countries have managed to put their fiscal houses in order by carefully saving foreign reserves. Latin America, beset in the past by sovereign defaults, currency devaluations, and the need for bailouts from rich countries, is experiencing solid economic growth that is the envy of first-world countries mired in stagnation or worse.

Figure 5: IMF's 2010 Projected GDP Growth Rates. (Source: World Economic Outlook. *World Economic and Financial Surveys,* October 2009, IMF. http://imf.org/external/pubs/ft/weo/2009/02/pdf/text.pdf)

China: 9.0%	France: 0.9%
India: 6.4%	UK: 0.9%
Brazil: 3.5%	Italy: 0.2%
Japan: 1.7%	Spain: –0.7%
USA: 1.5%	

Strong demand in Asia for commodities like iron ore, tin, and gold, and for foodstuffs like soy beans and meat, combined with policies in several Latin American economies that help control deficits and keep inflation low, are encouraging investment and propelling robust growth. After the crises of their "neoliberalized" economies they have tried not to be too vulnerable to the volatility of capital flows in the world. Now it is the turn of the developed economies to receive a prescription of the same medicine they purveyed to their poor brethren for so many years. On November 3, 2009, the International Monetary Fund warned the central countries, "While it is premature to begin exiting from fiscal support, governments should not hesitate to announce a credible exit strategy now."[1] It was in essence a call for fiscal austerity mindful, however, of the fact that premature austerity could kill recovery. Public authorities in these countries must navigate between a rock and a hard place. To recover from the financial crisis, they must dangerously increase the public debt; yet unsustainable debt leads to bankruptcy.

For the industrial nations unsustainable debt is a novel dilemma—however, not for Argentina, where it happened in 2001 and where it is no longer a problem; nor for little Iceland, which experienced the bankruptcy of its entire nation; nor for Sweden, where the near-insolvency of some Baltic republics has put Swedish banks at risk, nor for Dubai, which built ski slopes in the desert and shone itself as a capital of play money for the world, and today has a moratorium on payments. More seriously now, in some developed countries closer to the core of Europe, the possibility of sovereign debt default is not far off.

Greece is part of the European Union, and it is rapidly sliding down the slope toward default. Its budget deficit has exploded to 12.7 per cent of GDP, the worst in the 27 EU countries, while its outstanding public debt load is on track to hit 125 per cent of GDP in 2010. In order to avoid stiff EU penalties, Greece is slashing its operations budget by 10 per cent. The government is also planning a 2010 hiring lockdown and a partial public salary freeze. Greece's Finance Minister says there is "absolutely" no default risk. He sounds exactly like Argentina's Finance Minister in 2001. Meanwhile, Wall Street plays piñata with the potential Greek default, as it did with Argentina in 2001.[2]

Spain is in trouble because it experienced its own gigantic housing bubble, one that has long-since burst. Unemployment will top 20 per cent in 2010, while the nation's deficit is swelling toward 11 per cent of GDP. The economy has shrunk for six straight quarters, prompting the government to spend billions of euros to stimulate growth.[3]

Then there's the UK. Its budget deficit is running at 12 per cent of GDP, the highest in the Group of 20 leading nations. That is forcing the government to impose a 50 per cent tax on banker bonuses, and to boost income taxes. Despite those moves, the British Treasury is still going to have to borrow billions more pounds than it originally planned to fund its deficit.

Such predicaments once formed a familiar, and treacherous, territory for Latin Americans.[4] Today, however, for their former national masters of the IMF, chickens are coming home to roost.

During the heyday of this brave new world, historians Niall Ferguson and Moritz Schularick coined the word "Chimerica" to describe the combination of the Chinese and American economies. The expression aroused considerable interest among the chattering classes in both academic journals and the blogosphere. As these authors have recently reminded us, they chose the word because "we believed this relationship was a chimera —a monstrous hybrid like the part-lion, part-goat, part-snake of legend." They then appended an ominous afterthought, "Now we may be witnessing the death throes of the monster."[5]

The cause of this demise is simple: no line of credit is infinite, and Americans have exhausted theirs. From now on, they must consume less and save more, as they dig themselves out of the hole of accumulated debt. And indeed the economic crisis started in the financial sector and took the form of the drying up of credit. The immediate consequence was deflationary. Hence, the "desperate" measures of financial rescue and the various stimulus plans seek to re-inflate the economy and to restore trade.[6] Yet, the healing process will take considerable time, and in the best of all scenarios, rates of growth will be modest the world over. Rebalancing is the catchword.

What will this rebalancing look like in the various parts of the globe? What geopolitical de-couplings and new couplings will take place? The future is not uncharted territory, but it looks like a terrain of diverging paths. In this chapter, I will look at two of these paths: the future of Chimerica (China and America) which is the primary fork, and down the road, the implications of this primary rebalancing for a secondary fork, namely, the incipient association of China and the biggest Latin American economies. In short, I will show how "Chimerica" is giving way to "Chimericas."[7]

Let us start with the prospects for Chimerica. Who are the winners and losers in this unholy matrimony? As Ferguson and Schularick wrote, "With a combined 13 per cent of the world's land surface and around a quarter of its population, Chimerica nevertheless accounted for a third of global economic output and two-fifths of worldwide growth from 1998 to 2007." This is impressive. But if we disaggregate these figures and look at the differential impact on the partners, we arrive at the problematic heart of the matter.

For many consumer goods, China is surpassing the United States as the world's biggest market.[8] China is pulling ahead partly because Americans, debt-laden and jobless, are pulling back. After decades of over-consumption, Americans are saving. And the Chinese, whom economists thought were saving too much,[9] are spending more.

Among China's 1.3 billion people, rising incomes are finally making large numbers of Chinese prosperous enough to make important purchases. The Chinese government is increasing consumption with rebates, subsidies, and bank lending. Whether China can turn current spending into a true consumer society matters not just to China but to the world as a whole. Will the emerging consumer society be less exuberant and irrational in China than it has been in the US? Equality and sustainability are at stake here too.

The United States was able to maintain a high standard of living and the semblance of healthy growth (both in productivity and GDP) by outspending its national income and issuing debt in its own currency, a bonus that helped considerably in prolonging the simulacrum of prosperity. Having reached the sustainable limit of private indebtedness—now transferred to the public sector—it must reconvert the economy with strong public commitment to education and infrastructure to produce more real, not fictitious (superstructural) commodity counterparts in trade. In fairness, we must remember that despite the debt-fuelled bubble, the American economy remains the leader in information technology, biotechnology, and nearly every cutting-edge sector. It can continue to lead in several areas: aerospace, bio-medical inventions, alternative energies, and services, besides information and communication. All of these areas have a significant military component, which gives America an advantage, as the US continues to produce, albeit erratically, international security as a global public good. (I have no space here to discuss the morphing of old fashioned imperialism into global security.)[10]

For America, the challenge is considerable—an uphill socio-political battle in a downhill economic environment: how to get rid of past bad debt while stimulating the economy with new "good debt"?[11] During the giddy years of over consumption, the US neglected three crucial domains: basic education, general health, and physical infrastructure. Let us take education as an example. In the nineteenth century, public education in America was both a success and an inspiration to the world. A century and a half ago, Edward Everett—minister, scholar, politician, and president of Harvard University—asserted that the character of the nation was rooted in the idea of making "the care of the mind part of the public economy and the growth of knowledge a portion of the public wealth."[12] The plans and proposals of Horace Mann[13] inspired an Argentine statesman, Domingo Faustino Sarmiento, to institute the most successful program of primary and secondary education in South America, thus giving Argentina a prolonged advantage over her sister republics in human capital and overall economic performance. Fast forward to the twenty-first century: in 2006, ranking 15-year-olds from thirty industrialized countries, American teenagers placed a dismal twenty-first in science and twenty-fifth in mathematics. America as a whole has fallen behind, and the figures for Argentina are equally depressing.[14]

The phenomenon is neither novel nor unique, and comparative institutional economics offers some explanations. A century ago Thorstein Veblen sought to understand how some latecomers to the industrial world made rapid strides in machine technology and outstripped older powers from whom the modern industrial enterprise emanated. For the early comers the necessity of protecting the nominal capitalized values of investments obstructed their further growth in technical innovation. (This is the case of mature industrial societies like the US and older nations in Europe.) Veblen emphasized the negative influence of ownership structures and financial concentration.

Veblen maintained that some countries—i.e., Imperial Germany in Veblen's day (1915),[15] and the People's Republic of China today—avoided this "penalty of taking the lead" by virtue of their recent entrance to the group of the great powers. They are relatively free from the dead hand of funded capital. As a result, technology can develop at a faster pace than in the land of its birth.

Collective-action theorist Mancur Olson in *The Rise and Decline of Nations*[16] further elaborated the hypothesis but took it in a sociological direction. Olson's idea was that small distributional coalitions tend to form over time in countries. Groups like cotton-farmers, steel-producers, and labor unions have the incentives to form political lobbies and influence policies in their favor. These policies tend to be protectionist and anti-technology, and therefore hurt economic growth; but since the benefits of these policies are selective incentives concentrated among the few coalitions members, while the costs are diffused throughout the whole population, the "logic of collective action" dictates that there will be little public resistance to them. Hence, as time goes on, and these distributional coalitions accumulate in greater and greater numbers, the nation burdened by them will fall into economic decline. We can draw a practical corollary from the thesis. The difficulty of reform in the world of late Western capitalism lies in this: good policies are obstructed by bad politics, and politics is hobbled by the gridlock of vested interests.

China, on the other hand, profited from its lopsided relationship with America to build a formidable industrial base—probably the most impressive process of rapid industrialization ever undertaken in human history. Industrialization, in turn, brought hundreds of millions of poor peasants into the cities and into the ranks of the working class. It also generated a numerically enormous new middle class. China's marriage to America may have been a marriage of convenience destined not to last too long, but it was a means to develop Chinese society in all dimensions of the concept of capital—economic, social, cultural, and symbolic—beyond the wildest dreams of the most radical revolutionaries. Although Marx and Mao eulogized the revolutionary nature of capitalism, it would not have occurred to them that developmental communism would be an evolutionary stage in the progress toward a more advanced capitalist society. Yet it turned out to be precisely that, ever since Deng Xiao Ping and his team effected the Copernican turn in policy.

To be sure, Chinese progress has entailed large costs, and shows signs of structural stress: the environment is being ravaged; the government remains authoritarian if not totalitarian; the regime is brittle and overreacts to dissent or even to simple differences; human rights in the Western sense are not respected; the population is ageing. But the momentum of change is undeniable. To disengage from Chimerica will be a difficult and perhaps slow process. But it is also an exciting prospect, for it involves nothing else than further improving the standard of living of the large majority, and in directions more sustainable than the wasteful patterns of the overdeveloped West.

China could take a page from Brazil in this respect. Despite the reduction in poverty, China's Gini coefficient of income inequality is going up while Brazil's is coming down.[17] According to World Bank economist Francisco Ferreira, Brazil has shrunk its income gap by six percentage points since 2001, more than any other country in South America this decade. While the top 10 per cent of Brazil's earners saw their cumulative income rise by 7 per cent from 2001 to 2006, the bottom 10 per cent shot up by 58 per cent, according to Marcelo Côrtes Neri, the director of the Center for Social Policies at the Getulio Vargas Foundation in Rio de Janeiro.[18] In many ways, the country outclasses other BRICs. Unlike China, Brazil has embraced human rights, not only in the sense of democratic elections, but in terms of economic justice for African-Brazilians and indigenous peoples. Like the United States, Brazil was born in the crucible of slavery. Like the United States, it has come a long way. Even during the twentieth century, neither the indigenous populations nor the African-Brazilian slave descendants had much chance in the economic and social order. That has changed. Public education is becoming universally available, including for groups that faced harsh discrimination in the past. Targeted social programs are reducing the income gaps and giving a sense of empowerment to those at the bottom of the social pyramid.

Brazilian elites seem to have understood that there are big differences in growth strategies, and that the first difference concerns how growth itself is conceived. Growth is not just a matter of increasing GDP. It must be sustainable; growth based on environmental degradation, a debt-financed consumption binge, or the exploitation of scarce natural resources, without reinvesting the proceeds, is not sustainable. Both the Cardoso and the Lula administrations in Brazil have had the sincere conviction that growth, while a worthy objective, must be inclusive as well, so that a majority of citizens benefit. A mere increase in GDP can actually leave most citizens worse off. The "Brazilian miracle" of growth under the military regime that lasted more than twenty years (1964–1985) inaugurated the habit of long-range *national* public policies,[19] but it was neither economically sustainable nor inclusive. That fortunately changed after democracy was restored.

There need not be a trade-off between inequality and growth. Failures to promote social solidarity can have other costs, not the least of which are the social and private expenditures required to protect property and incarcerate criminals (this problem still plagues Brazil and is a consequence of previous unsustainable growth).[20] Conversely, greater equality promotes solidarity and can enhance growth. There is considerable empirical research that supports this strategy. The empirical basis for this conception stems from the analysis of comparative economic success: among the older developed nations there are the cases of Germany and Japan; among the newly industrialized countries, the combination of high growth and low inequality is remarkable in Hong Kong, Singapore, and Taiwan. These countries deliberately set out to spread the effects of growth.

Among developing countries, there is an inverse correlation between inequalities of income and growth.[21] The cost of inequality in repression alone can hinder growth.[22] In Brazil a year in prison can cost more than a year at an exclusive private college. The costs of violence and social dysfunction—and of measures undertaken to repress or contain them should be viewed as subtractions from GDP, not as add-ons. In the Brazilian state of São Paulo, there were more than 2,176 reported resistance killings over a five-year period (2004–2009), according to Human Rights Watch, an international monitoring organization—in contrast with the 1,623 police killings over the same period in South Africa, a country with a much higher homicide rate. In fairness we must say that the Brazilian administration has embarked on a strong campaign to "retake" city slums from criminal gangs, as part of a larger policy of targeted development in the same urban areas.

For China, a Brazilian strategy will be good for the masses and good for the economy, as China weans itself from the addiction to exports and shifts its focus to what in the past made America great. There seems to be awareness of such necessity. For it is apt to remember, as one drives through the industrial ruins of cities like Detroit, that America was once a country that made tangible products, put people to work, and paid them decent wages, a place where mass production for the home market was also a school to the world, and the cradle of the modern middle class. A shift to internal markets, and the embrace of democratic rights would signal the next step in big change for China.[23]

During this transition to a more complete and prosperous industrial society, and after the shift as well, China will find other partners to trade with, to produce goods and services with, and to exchange people and ideas with. Some of these partners are and will continue to be other Asian nations, but many others will be the wider global South, among them many Latin American countries. And this opens up the prospect of a more complex and dynamic multi-polar world: China and the Americas—the Chimericas.

There are some countries in Latin America that are ready to enter this special relationship, and some have already started. As Argentine economist Carlos Garramón has argued, commodity-rich countries in the Americas are strategically positioned for another round of export growth pulled by the Chinese locomotive, which will replace America as an engine of world economic recovery.[24] The Southern Cone of the continent produces one third of the grains consumed worldwide; it produces half the meat exported around the world (a market that will increase as the standard of living of Asian populations rises); and it has energy reserves (oil, gas, and bio-fuels) that rival those under Arab soil. As an example, thirty per cent of the copper consumed by China already comes from Chile. Moreover, the region has a continent-size country which, like China two decades ago, has "awaken" from a long historic slumber: Brazil. It is a regional force already, and it is one of the more attractive of the BRICs: economically diversified, politically stable, and democratic to boot—with all the advantages of the economies of scale. Its new middle classes will stimulate, through their consumption, neighboring economies that will coalesce around the Brazilian pole. At the same time, Brazil will maintain generally good relations with the United States, acting both as a buffer and a broker in the more contentious issues that beset the continent. Additionally, Brazil and the other countries of the Southern Cone have weathered the world financial crisis with their economic houses in order. For them, the world crisis has been more a setback in trade than a financial meltdown.

Garramón concludes, and I concur with his prognosis, as follows:

> The near future for the Southern Cone is promising, the recovery will arrive earlier and will manifest itself in 2010 in growth rates in the order of 3 to 4 per cent. This year, Brazil initiated its recovery and capital inflows and foreign investment are being restored; Uruguay is one of few countries in the world that will show a slightly positive growth rate in 2009; Argentina has reverted its capital flight and is leaving behind the constraining effects of its default and its debt with the Paris Club. We are approaching a promising 2010. In order to consolidate these trends it will be necessary to acknowledge that China is the strategic partner par excellence for Latin America's Southern Cone, and based on this conclusion, to accordingly coordinate the region's trade policy.[25]

As opposed to Chimerica, the Chimericas are not a chimera. To support this hypothesis, I will offer an additional proof *a contrario*—that is, the Mexican post-crisis situation (treated at greater length in another chapter).

Since the opening up of its former rigid political system, and the simultaneous opening of its economy through the North American Free Trade Association (NAFTA), Mexico has tied its fate ever more closely to that of the United States. The resulting interdependence of the two countries has been at best a mixed blessing, and at worst, as with the current American slump, a drag on Mexico's potential. In the past, when Mexico succumbed to an endogenous crisis, the United States came to the rescue. Mexico then pulled out of its troubles by putting itself on the American dole. In the present, when Mexico succumbed to a financial crisis generated in the United States, it cannot pull itself out of the hole. The situation is made worse by the fact that, while the bilateral relation with the US was moving forward, Mexico postponed or avoided necessary reforms, and thus cut itself off from alternative paths of growth. NAFTA left Mexico highly dependent on the health of the American economy. The treatise brought a lot of American investment as manufacturers set up plants south of the border to make use of lower labor costs: *maquilas,*[26] car companies, construction, and tourism buttressed Mexican growth, but the input was almost exclusively American. As these were the very sectors hardest hit by the recession, exports plummeted, transport suffered, and even the flow of remittances from Mexicans in the US dwindled when the US economy did not go into reverse. As opposed to Brazil and some of the other countries in the southern cone, Mexico was quick to enter into a recession and will be longer to exit from it. As the country looks for other partners to boost its growth, it finds itself at a disadvantage, due to its previous neglect of ties other than those to the United States. In the end, NAFTA has proven to be chimerical,[27] while the Chimericas are becoming a reality.

Not only did NAFTA bring little change to the domestic economy of Mexico; it made it possible for its entrenched monopolies and its oligopolies and its hidebound labor organizations to hamper internal growth when it has been most needed. Mexico's tight embrace of the United States has isolated it from sister republics to the south and from a wider, rising world. In the end, there will be reform and rebalance here too, but it will be a longer and more painful process than in many other parts of Latin America. For the moment however, it is springtime in Brasilia, and winter in Aztec land.

Chapter Six

OTHER CAPITALISMS: WHAT LATIN AMERICANS CAN LEARN FROM THOSE WHO DO IT WELL

Among the first public buildings we know of from the earliest civilizations are granaries. They were used to provide emergency relief in years when crops failed. We remember the story of Joseph advising Pharaoh to build up a store of grain because the seven good years would be followed by seven years of famine. This is ancient wisdom: we should save when times are good so as to be prepared for hard times.

Over the last year, the world has experienced the most severe economic crisis since the 1930s.

This international crisis has also affected Norway. We have a small, open economy, and half of what we produce is sold abroad. When export markets disappear, people at home are hit. Some of those who used to manufacture car components, smelt aluminum or build ships lost their jobs because people abroad stopped buying these goods.

Losing a job is first and foremost a blow for the person concerned. But unemployment also harms the community. With fewer people producing goods, there is less to go round. During this crisis, we have injected a great deal of extra funds to keep the wheels in motion. We have been able to spend more during these difficult times because we were careful when times were good. In this respect, you could say that we have followed the advice Joseph gave to Pharaoh, albeit in a rather different way. The Egyptians built granaries. We built the Government Pension Fund Global.

Norway
Prime Minister Jens Stoltenberg
New Year's Address, 1 January 2010

It is important for Latin Americans to look at Scandinavia for alternative models that address social inequality while maintaining the spark of capitalist invention and adaptability. Why? For cultural and historical reasons, a radical critique of capitalism will always find wide support in Latin America. But the popular critique fails to notice however that there is not one capitalism but many, and that radical alternatives have failed. The critics often discard the baby together with the bath water and entertain wild fantasies about the alternatives.

In the field of sustainable development (not fitful growth as in Latin America) with social inclusion (development for all and not just a few), there is much to learn from successful experiences in other latitudes. These experiences however, cannot simply be imported like an automobile. The first step in taking advantage of lessons from abroad is cutting through the rhetoric associated with particular models and looking at the mid- and long-term results of public investment. The second step is examining the social base and political/institutional consensus that surround such state policies.[1]

An Excursion to Other Lands

I have spent four summers visiting Scandinavia, sailing along its coasts. First came the North Sea, which I traced along the fjords of Norway, reaching the Arctic Circle and beyond. I even reached the legendary *Ultima Thule* (the northernmost region of the habitable world as thought of by ancient geographers). Then I visited Finland. I was able to traverse the Gulf of Bothnia (the northern arm of the Baltic Sea) from Finland to Sweden, before finally returning to Finland the Aland Islands. I also learned to read and decipher a few phrases in Swedish and Norwegian.

In Norway, I grew interested in a topic of strategic significance: How can a country profit from its oil reserves without also corrupting its customs and institutions? I visited oil wells and platforms and interviewed common citizens, oil workers, and business executives in Oslo, Stavanger, and Bergen, and along the length of a coast that extends to extreme northern latitudes. In Sweden, I became interested in how the country, in the 1990s, emerged relatively unscathed from a financial crisis similar to the one that stunned the world in 2008 and 2009, albeit on a smaller scale. I spent time in Oregrund, traveled to the ancient university city of Uppsala where I visited libraries, the tomb of Swedenborg, and the Linnaeus gardens. In Finland, in turn, I asked myself (and anyone whom I was able to interview) how a small, sparsely populated country with strong agricultural roots was able to leap to the vanguard of the postindustrial world and compete globally with high-tech products. More recently I visited Denmark. According to the polls, it has the happiest population on the planet. Apparently the Danes are highly productive and freethinking and move between jobs without the slightest trepidation. My ultimate goal is to assemble a collective vision of the Nordic countries. At this stage in my research I can already anticipate a few conclusions, enumerated below with an eye to helping Latin America.

The Value of the Concrete

Ideologies obfuscate because they present mere abstractions as real things. These abstractions, in turn, become idols for the tribe, adored and abhorred and, in general, feared. They generate closed and antagonistic camps. In the heat of the battle, these camps abandon good sense and come to prefer fervor and delirium to everyday realities. All of the "-isms" that bombard us in public discourse or in social chatter simplify the world, distort it, stylize it in antagonistic capsules that divide people and end up becoming rallying cries for struggles as ferocious as they are futile. The last century was a graveyard of "-isms": fascism, communism, Nazism, liberalism, etc. Almost all perished, but the twenty-first century has given rise to another round of "-isms": neoliberalism, twenty-first-century socialism, fundamentalism, terrorism, and so on. The contents and the packaging changes; the social function remains the same.

The only effective way to overcome these illusions is not through conflict in the streets or on the fields but through deconstruction. By deconstruction I mean the patient work of dismantling the scarecrows, which in ideological discourse we call "models." In Latin America, some politicians denounce the insidious models imposed on the continent by the dominant countries. Others defend their own political or economic "models." Truth be told, these models are rarely more than pretentious guises used to cover up a mediocre leadership style.

The first step in effective deconstruction is to bring these models face-to-face with the complexity of reality. For instance, we must recognize—as has English historian Eric Hobsbawm—that "socialism failed and capitalism is bankrupt." And then we need to ask ourselves, "What next?"[2] Out of the rubble of the "-isms," we can glean many things: valuable lessons about what works and is worthwhile, and cautionary tales about what doesn't work or shouldn't be attempted. Emulate, invent, adapt, and avoid. These verbs have replaced—at least, in many regions—the ardent verbs of other eras: join, struggle, resist, triumph, and die. The heroism of the late twentieth and the early twenty-first centuries is quiet and persistent: protecting the environment, reducing suffering, eradicating sickness, bringing about reconciliation, and finding concrete solutions. In the light of these patient labors, the furious, garish heroism of bygone eras—the conquer-or-die mentality—seems little more than a mask hiding sordid interests and base appetites. It produces much more suffering that it purports to palliate.

The second step in effective deconstruction is to abandon abstractions and to look at concrete examples. One good approach is to simply pluralize the idea of the "model." For instance, think in terms of capitalisms in the plural and not "capitalism" *tout court*. In other words, abandon the singular, universal model in favor of a plurality of regional models, which can, in turn, be broken down into national models. This approach involves setting aside abstract schemes and focusing instead on the distinct experiences that go into building a society, an economy, and a country.

Nordic Experiences

Just as there is no one model of capitalism, there is no single Nordic model. Norway, Denmark, Sweden, and Finland (we might also include Holland in this list) have many things in common but each is also unique in important respects. They are capitalist countries in the broad sense of the term, and they share a noteworthy achievement: Each enjoys an inclusive, market economy that minimizes poverty, and an efficient state involved in egalitarian policies. In all of these countries, taxation and public spending are high and the network of social protections is broad, as one would expect in a welfare state. But neither such spending nor these measures stop these countries from innovating, producing, and competing in global markets. Their labor markets are relatively free but subject to active public policies. Unions are strong but, rather than posing an obstacle to business dynamism, work together with management. The Northern countries seek to bring together efficiency and equity.[3]

When pundits speak of the Nordic model, they often compare it with the Anglo-Saxon experience in the United States, the United Kingdom and Ireland, countries where equity and efficiency have marched along steadily diverging paths. In these places distrust of the state is deep-seated, and inequality, neglect of the needy, and poverty have grown progressively worse. But the level of dynamism, productivity and efficiency is very high. The neoliberal model refers to attempts to impose the Anglo-Saxon experience on very different countries at crucial moments in their historical trajectory. The Washington consensus of the 1990s references the moment when the countries of Latin America and other regions, in the throes of economic and social crisis, sought assistance from the US, which had assumed the role of the world's only superpower. The diagnosis that these countries received was not completely flawed, but it would prove nearly fatal. To draw a comparison, neoliberalism was like a remedy recommended for a certain illness before the advent of antibiotics. Syphilis, for example, was "cured" by injecting the patient with a strong dose of malaria.

Other capitalist countries have even less favorable combinations of policies and institutions. For instance, France protects, with the collaboration of small but strategic trade unions, the employed at the expense of the jobless (above all, young people and immigrants), who are kept from fully entering society by daunting barriers. It is a country where unionism and progressive-ism are buttresses of privilege and not engines of equity.[4] In the area of the Mediterranean, countries such as Italy, Spain, Greece, and also Atlantic Portugal lavish public spending on pensions and maintain employment levels by sacrificing the labor flexibility necessary in a modern and competitive world. In sum, these countries pay for equity and social protection with a kind of economic arthritis and a structural deficit in the public ledger.[5]

What exactly are the most notable achievements logged by the Nordic capitalisms? Except for the unemployment rate, the figures in all aggregate charts are encouraging, although performance in some categories has suffered with the global economic crisis affecting everyone. The Nordic countries show that it is possible, in practice, to overcome one of the greatest challenges of sustainable development: to combine aspirations for greater economic prosperity with a high degree of social protection.[6] For politicians and economists of other latitudes who have long debated how to reconcile market forces with guarantees against insecurity and the anguish of social exclusion, the achievements of the Nordic countries should indeed represent a kind of Holy Grail.

But there is more. In general, Nordic economies perform better than economies in English-speaking countries. Only Norway is below them on the scale (Fig. 6), but still close to Hong Kong, perhaps due to resource dependence.

Figure 6: List of the World's Most Competitive Economies. (Source: World Economic Forum)

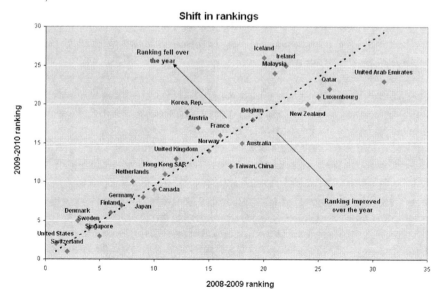

The Nordic countries sustain a high level of economic dynamism in spite of an elevated tax burden. Social spending there is compatible with an open, competitive, market-based economy. "Capitalism" and "socialism" are not opposing concepts but modules that can be combined in different ways. It is important to ask why, in these countries, public spending does not hinder economic growth? Why haven't high taxes killed private incentive and the thirst for improvement? Why hasn't the incorporation of disadvantaged sectors proved a burden for everyone else? The answers to these questions lead to some very valuable insights, above all for the countries of the global South.

Learning Without Copying

If we combine the characteristics of the Nordic countries into a single "model," we end up with little more than a Utopian vision, impossible to achieve in the South. On the other hand, if we break the model into discrete pieces, we can take away useful lessons adaptable to our setting, particularly in terms of the goals of public policies.

First, it is not public spending that should frighten us, and reducing spending at any cost (the order of the day in Washington and other capitals of the rich world) is the wrong approach. The key lies in where the spending is applied. There is purely redistributive spending, deficit spending, and inflationary spending. In general, these contribute in the end to social hardship. But there is also non-inflationary spending (although this may come in the form of deficit spending) that brings economic and social returns in the middle and longer terms. We should therefore learn to see non-inflationary spending as a good investment. Here the Nordic lesson is very clear: Both in times of boom and bust, countries like Finland have maintained high and consistent levels of public spending on health and education, and public investment in infrastructure. Medical coverage embraces the entire population. (The Finns spend 7 per cent of their GDP on healthcare services, which are excellent and widely available, while the US spends 17 per cent of their GDP on far spottier services.) Education is public and free at all levels, from kindergarten to professional studies, with a particular emphasis on the expansion of technical institutes. Comparing this strategy to strategies in other countries—including some European Union members—is telling (though it may appear a bit unfair).

Let me offer a simple comparison. There are two small cities in Europe with exactly the same population: 32,000 people. In lovely Lucca, in the heart of Tuscany, there are 300 Catholic churches and several monasteries, two nursery schools, a high school and a music school. After much struggle, my colleagues and I were able to establish an institute for advanced studies in technical and social sciences that, to this day, is viewed with distrust by the locals. In the more austere city of Kokkola, Finland, on the other hand, there are only two Lutheran churches, several primary schools and five technical schools. These schools produce highly qualified graduates who work in small- and medium-sized high-tech businesses in the region (shipyards, marine engines, computers, steel rollers, and paper mills). In Kokkola the Protestant ethic and a business spirit predominate; in Lucca the Catholic ethic and the humanist spirit predominate. Both cities once depended heavily on the production of paper pulp. But today Lucca is preserved by tourism in a mummified state, while Kokkola continues to search for industrial innovation. In the end, Finnish public spending stimulates economic development, promotes equality, and accelerates social mobility. There is no significant poverty, and life expectancy surpasses that in the US.

Let us move from Finland to South America. Here, it is important to point out that if Argentina has not slipped even further in world economic rankings it is because its population enjoys a level of education and training superior to its neighbors. One hundred and fifty years after the fact, the educational policies and public investments of an enlightened elite continue to benefit everyone, despite the slippage of the country to third world status.

Another Nordic virtue with strategic value should be highlighted: the countries' unyielding commitment to scientific research and the development of new, high-tech products. The Finns dedicate 3.5 per cent of their domestic product to R&D. The Swedes dedicate no less than 4.3 per cent of theirs to the same task. The Nordic people understand that in order to maintain a comfortable place in a globalized world it is not enough to simply look inward. It is necessary to compete globally with high-quality, value-added products. An important and growing part of the spending of the Nordic government is dedicated to financing research and its commercial applications. In Finland, funds are channeled through a public agency, Tekes, which supports both pure and applied research both in universities (40 per cent) and in private businesses (60 per cent). In 2009, Tekes spent $540 million this way—some $10,000 for every Finnish citizen. If the US did the same, it would be spending $300 billion dollars each year on research and development.

All of these accomplishments—and there are many others—share a key element that is neither technical nor economic but rather social, political, and geopolitical. All of the Nordic countries have small, relatively homogeneous populations (although this is changing with immigration, which is in turn linked to the aging of the population) with a broad consensus on public and state policies. They also occupy a geopolitical position that has left them on the sidelines of the great global conflicts. Ultimately, these are the variables that we, in the global South, must consider before we try to glean any benefits from the Nordic model. But the lesson is clear. In the uneven recovery from the world crisis, Latin American countries should take advantage of their favorable position in order to build the human and infrastructural basis for a better future. So far in 2010, emerging markets are still barreling their way to a strong performance despite the problems that have beset advanced economies. In a long-term structural sense, they are becoming less dependent on advanced economies. It's true—emerging markets cannot pull the world economy along by themselves. If advanced economies continue to turn in a weak performance, we are in for a long and hard slog towards a durable global economic recovery. But then, never mind the slog in the lands of the rich. *Carpe diem*: the global South can seize the moment to undertake its own bold endeavors.

Chapter Seven

RETHINKING LATIN AMERICAN DEPENDENCY

The world wire services have recently reported that China has agreed to invest about $10 billion over several years to renovate Argentina's dilapidated railway system and build a subway for Rosario—its second-largest city.[1] To expedite the export of beef and wheat to Europe the British had built Argentina's once-extensive rail network a century ago.[2] It was nationalized by Perón in the late forties (when it was already in disrepair and largely obsolete), and dismantled during the neoliberal privatizations of the 1990s. But as agricultural output soars, farmers and the operators of grain elevators—who send more than 80 per cent of grains by costly road transport—have been calling for investment to revive the railways. Mark Twain was right: history may not repeat itself, but sometimes it rhymes. China in recent years has been funding infrastructure projects in emerging economies that bolster relations and further Beijing's own economic goals by helping bring goods and raw materials to market faster. One has a sense of *déjà vu*.

There is no better time than the present crisis to dust off the old theory of dependency and draw from it those points that remain relevant. Latin Americans need to think about which ties to sever and which to strengthen. The fate of thought is a curious thing—above all in times of crisis. As the current crisis continues along its destructive path, some regions have been more affected then others, oftentimes in defiance of prevailing wisdom. This represents something new.

Crisis and Criteria

Until recently, neoliberal thinkers maintained that those places without "good economic foundations" (as defined by their theories) engendered or would engender financial crises.[3] Nonetheless, the present crisis broke out among the "good" teachers before it affected the bad pupils. In Latin America, many of the countries that earned high marks during the neoliberal era or that benefited from global economic growth now find themselves in bad straits and risk losing the gains of the past ten years. The current crisis has put "good" and "bad" countries on the same footing and even inverted traditional hierarchies. Just like it says in the tango *Cambalache*: *"Dale nomas! Dale que va! Que allá en el horno/nos vamo a encontrar "* (Go ahead! Keep it up! That there, in hell/we're gonna reunite).

To what factors can we attribute Latin America's unexpected good economic performance over the last decade? Answering this question requires keeping in mind not only the productive capacity of the economic system but also, and more importantly, the system's structure and those factors that determine that structure. To this end, we need to revisit the "made in Latin America" theories, which date back thirty to fifty years and are widely considered obsolete, when not forgotten altogether. This global crisis has led many people to turn to older economists for guidance. It is useful to look back on two currents of Latin American thought: structuralism and the dependency theory. In them there are some good guidelines for interpreting the current situation. First, I will review the main ideas from these old theories and see if they remain valid. Second, I will evaluate the current global crisis from the perspective of the original proponents of these theories. Third, I will speculate on how the crisis may play out.

The Life and Death of Dependency Theory

"Dependency and development" was a catchphrase in the 1970s. It was the name given to a theory with both empirical and normative components. The ultimate decline of this theory had a lot to do with certain public policies that were derived from it and which seem ill-advised in retrospect. Nonetheless, the theory also had a positive side and still provides a valuable analytical framework. Without delving into the evolution of the dependency theory,[4] consider its principal propositions:

- The structure of the world economy is divided into central countries and peripheral countries. Processes and policies in the central countries structure economic development in peripheral countries. In other words, some countries can choose and control their development path while others are compelled to follow suit. In an early formulation, "The interdependency between two or more economies, and between these economies and global commerce, takes the form of dependency when some countries— the dominant ones—can grow in a self-sustained fashion, while other countries—the dependent ones—can only grow in response to expansion in the former countries, which has both positive and negative effects on immediate development in these dependent countries."[5]

- Underdevelopment is different from undevelopment. At some point in time, the developed countries were undeveloped. Their economic potential was not exploited. Nonetheless, they had a high degree of autonomy and the possibility of following a course of sustained economic growth. Underdeveloped countries, however, found themselves in a different position. Even if they fully exploited their productive capacity, these countries found the direction of development predetermined by the characteristics of the international exchange system. To cite the poet Antonio Machado, the developed countries "made the path by walking it." The underdeveloped countries followed that path laid by the developed countries. In one respect, dependency theory is a theory of sequencing in economic history. Another way of expressing this idea would be to say that the developed countries found the right components of structure for their system, while the underdeveloped countries became trapped in a system created by someone else.[6] The necessities of the first-developed countries speed up or delay, promote or repress, the development of distinct sectors (countries, regions) in the periphery. The issue is not so much deliberately imposed obstacles or impediments to development (since at times the needs of the most developed countries facilitate the growth of the least developed) but of exogenous necessities as the driving force.[7]
- The structural dependency scheme condemns underdeveloped countries to follow the economic ups and downs of the central countries. A recession in the metropole logically affects the satellites, slowing their growth.
- Dependency is perpetuated and reproduced on various levels. It is not merely a rigid division between center and periphery but also an asymmetry of power, which constitutes its political dimension. Dependency depends, for instance, on the existence of local elites with strong ties to the center. In the words of Vincent Ferraro, "these elites have trained in the dominant states and share cultural values with the elites in the dominant countries. In this way, the dependency relation is to a certain degree "voluntary." There is no need to argue that the elites of a dependent state intentionally betray the interests of the poor; the elites sincerely believe that the key to development lies in following the liberal economic doctrine."[8] In this way, dependency exists through a web of relations.
- Dependency favors the central countries. They can sell their products in peripheral markets and, at the same time, access natural resources. The relation is maintained through a complex network of political, cultural, economic, and military means.
- When the dependency relation lessens, the peripheral countries have a better shot at development.[9] This opening occurs in times of crisis in the metropolis. The best-known examples are severe economic depression

and war. The ties of dependency generally tighten once again once these emergencies are over.

All of these propositions have a strong normative charge, which is why they have given rise to resistance movements and anti-imperialist drives. But it is important to focus on the thesis itself and test it empirically. If underdevelopment is inevitable in a system of dependency, then it would follow that relative economic isolation would be a prerequisite to sustainable development. The following are some of the practical recommendations that grow out of dependency theory, which experience has made questionable:

- Development should accord with national interest. Given that underdeveloped countries have an initial disadvantage in their markets (above all, in terms of industrial production) the state should address this weakness through aggressive and extensive intervention.
- One of the most important concrete initiatives is state-sponsored stimulus for strategic industries. This is not a matter of exploiting "natural" comparative advantages but of creating new enterprises with comparative advantages.
- A recommended strategy is the development of the domestic market by substituting imported manufactured goods with domestic ones.
- For dependency theorists, since foreign investment drains away added value and moves resources out of Latin America, they recommend the nationalization of key economic sectors.

The development of many Latin American countries over the last forty years has discredited some of these recommendations of dependency theorists. Ironically, however, the performance of the Asian Tigers (South Korea, Taiwan, and others) seems to offer some empirical proof of the dependency theory. In these countries, the state adopted strategies that accord closely with the prescriptions of dependency theorists.

In Latin America however, there was no shortage of cases that disproved the theory. The critical backlash was severe, above all with respect to the flawed import substitution model of industrialization (ISI). It is hard to deny the importance of free trade to the growth of all of Latin America. But the neoliberal critique leaves a lot out of the picture. Neoliberals have not been able to explain the structural problems noted by dependency theorists, nor the leaps in development that occur in Southern countries when Northern countries are in crisis.

Within dependency theory there are a number of distinct positions. The "softest" have strong explanatory power. Back in 1978, Fernando Henrique Cardoso was talking about "associated-dependent development" as a model that conferred many benefits. In spite of Cardoso telling his intellectual friends to "forget everything I have written" when he assumed the presidency of Brazil, his policies and those of his successor Luiz Inácio Lula da Silva have supported an associated-dependent development model that has raised Brazil to the threshold of world power. In sum, today, in the midst of severe global crisis, the arguments of neoliberal economists are losing strength and some elements of the old theory of dependency are again attracting interest.

A Brief History of Crises

Throughout the seventies, the growth rate in many Latin American countries was quite high. Many had applied some of the recommendations derived from dependency theory, in particular the important substitution model. It looked at the time like this was an effective strategy for escaping the trap of dependency.

However, these recommendations ignored changes happening in the global economy. They represented solutions to problems from other eras. While the big ideas behind dependency theory were not flawed, its practical corollaries were. In other words, there had been a good diagnosis but a bad treatment plan. The main error was in Latin America's trying to isolate itself from the rest of the world in a bubble of self-sufficiency in place of creatively adapting to a changing scene. The way to break the cycle of dependence was not through independence but through interdependence. This was the secret behind the success of many Asian economies. Latin America, on the other hand, became mired in short-term policies and in economic nationalism. And, for those reasons Latin American countries missed two important changes in the world economy: the abandonment of the gold standard and the amassing of Middle Eastern oil profits, which were subsequently turned into loans for Latin America. The abandonment of the gold standard enabled the US to dominate the global economy without worrying about its own reserves. Instead, the US currency became everyone else's reserve. The South American countries used the dollar as a reference currency. They contracted huge debts in dollars, which the US, in turn, happily injected all over the planet. At the same time, massive profits earned by petroleum exporting countries were being converted to loans for other countries rather than being earmarked for local economic development.

These changes affected Latin American countries in two ways. First, Latin America became the principal target of lenders (the Western banks). Capital flowed into South America in large amounts. The cycle of indebtedness began and would ultimately conclude with huge crises and sorrow. Rather than achieving interdependence, the Latin American countries fell prey to international financial interests.

This new dependency was very similar to what in the Northern Hemisphere is known as a Ponzi scheme and in the Southern Hemisphere a "chain," that is, a serial fraud: New loans pay off old loans until the chain breaks leaving a long line of victims behind. Initially, gains are spectacular, but the fictitious wealth quickly tumbles like a house of cards. Easy access to financial capital undermined the bases of development in Latin America. Corruption, moral jeopardy, and bankruptcy were the final results. The system of financial dependency entered its terminal phase in 1982. The crisis was followed by a "lost decade." Then the economies recovered by following neoliberal guidelines, generally poorly applied, which brought first a boom and then a bust of epic proportions at the beginning of the twenty first century. Multilateral organizations—instead of mitigating the crisis—exacerbated it, which explains the ill repute of these bodies in the region today.

This brief review of Latin American crises has a purpose: It is necessary to contemplate these earlier crises in order to understand the possibilities opened by the current crisis and to avoid repeating the mistakes of the past. It is also important to consider the underlying causes of the earlier crises. The first underlying cause was the weakness of financial markets in the region, which failed to attract the capital needed to stimulate healthy and sustained development. The second cause was the volatility of the resources, or commodities, that was Latin America exporting. These countries were at the mercy of the ups and downs of commodities, both hard and soft. Speculative capital came in and then left with the same ease that characterized its predatory entry. Fluctuations in the prices of exportable resources, in turn, made the economies vulnerable. The countries moved with astonishing alacrity from a festive mood when prices rose, to regret and insolvency with prices fell. How could they break this vicious cycle of multiple dependencies?

The current global crisis, on account of its planetary reach, offers an opportunity. The decline in the flow of volatile capital prods the countries of the region to seek new forms of regional collaboration and a new outlook that favors development that is local, integrated, and sustained.

New Opportunities

It would be naive to pretend that the global crisis, all by itself, will lead to a new era of economic interdependence. In addition, in some respects certain threads of dependence have already been severed. The unfettered influence of international financial capital has been restrained. Combine this with the power now accessible to new political forces, and we can look forward to a new period of pragmatic experimentation. It is also clear that the crisis will drain capital from Latin America. But at the same time the dominance of capital from Northern countries will be weakened. The prognosis remains unsettled, but there is no reason to rule out positive possibilities. The need for financing may oblige Latin American countries to once again go knocking at the door of multilateral bodies for assistance, with the ensuing conditions and dependency that we all know too well. However, there are ways to avoid the dependency trap.

One way is to secure lines of credit but not use them, an approach already taken by several countries. This produces confidence in capital markets but does not generate dependency. Furthermore, developing countries are currently in a position to negotiate the conditions imposed by Northern lenders. Another option is to create regional capital poles to stimulate local development. The objective here is to break the North's monopoly on financial capital. As a third option, the role of the state can be very important during the exit from the crisis, and state intervention (if intelligent) will encounter less resistance than before, as all global economies have had to recur to state assistance. Intelligent fiscal policies will prove decisive in this area. Taxation policies, incentives for local investment, and other development-oriented mechanisms will pave the way for reform. In many cases, further development will be financed by new debt—but this time good debt. Other alternatives include the creation of local and regional capital funds, with specific financial strategies, to stimulate local investment.

In our current interdependent times, to pursue a course of self-sufficiency would be disastrous. I will even dare to say that dependent development is preferable to economic isolation. "*Vivir con lo nuestro*" (to live with one's own) is neither possible nor desirable. We must learn to distinguish instead between the various degrees and types of dependency.

There is no doubt that current reality has rendered obsolete old propositions that were based on an earlier model of international division of labor, terms of exchange, and comparative advantages. In the 1950s for instance, the thesis developed independently by economists Raul Prebisch and Hans Singer, suggested that countries that export commodities (such as most developing countries) would be able to import fewer and fewer manufactured goods for a given level of exports.

Nowadays the distinction between primary products (or natural resources) and manufactured products has been blurred. The primary products of yesteryear are now subject to an industrial production and processing. Comparative advantages are created and do not just "happen." And, with good strategy, the terms of exchange can be reversed. All of this was understood rather well in Asian countries. But the wisdom was slow to reach Latin American shores. The real distinction is between specific products (which can yield comparative advantages) and substitutable products, which will forever be at the mercy of demand and require the support of protectionist policies, with negative results in the long run.

This modernization of strategic thought has also been absent from the views of Latin American critics of dependency. We know that a strategy influenced by dependency theory is not conceivable in a neoliberal framework, but it is also difficult to imagine it within the so-called economic nationalism currently espoused by some of Latin America's self-styled "progressive" governments. There is something worse than dependence, and that is a poorly conceived independence. In other words, the loosening of the bonds of dependency that the international crisis has initiated is merely an opportunity and not a guarantee for the Southern countries. As in all crises, the margin of error is large.

A Note on Hostile Dependency: Venezuela

The arrival of a leftist government in Venezuela has not altered the basic condition of dependency. The change in political regime has been significant, and its defiance of the United States quite strident. And yet Venezuela today depends on oil revenues as much as before. The state-oil company has become the center of a command economy, albeit such command is the rule of one man who has consolidated power and redistributes income to maintain his popular support. Hugo Chávez uses this power as a platform to defy the greatest power on earth and to seduce or cajole other governments in the region to do the same. But without the demand of the global economy sustaining the adventure everything would fall down.

Oil did not undo democracy in Venezuela. It constituted and sustained it from the beginning, and corrupted it as it went along. Oil was present at the birth of a redistributive state and shaped the formation of a two-party system that shared the spoils. It fostered not a work ethic but a culture of rent entitlements that seeped deeply into the habits of all levels of society. The cultural dependency on a natural bonanza with its own sense of 'just' and 'unjust' returns produced a paradox: widespread corruption and inefficiencies in public institutions were tolerated as long as the boom continued, but provoked popular indignation at those same institutions when the oil spigot was closed or its flow slowed down to a trickle. Oil both helped the installation of democracy and undermined its legitimacy. Under such circumstances, the cyclical nature of oil dependency resulted in a political scenario not unlike that described by Karl Marx in *The Eighteenth Brumaire of Louis Bonaparte*.[10] A corrupt democratic system that depended on multiple payoffs could not weather well a serious economic downturn, and ultimately succumbed to a new form of Caesaristic arbitration with popular support. It opened the gates to what Max Weber called *Plebzitaeren Fueher Demokratie* (plebiscitary leader democracy),[11] which paradoxically is underpinned by the same oil revenues as the system that it replaced, with one caveat: It can easily turn into a repressive dictatorship when faced with serious adversity.

In Venezuela's case, democratic backsliding has this peculiar form: oil democracy is inherently corruptible and fragile. It has few resources to manage crises. Its successor (populist) regime is also corruptible but capable of repressive countermeasures that are absent in a democratic system. Oil has given Venezuelans the means to engage in two historical projects that seem doomed to failure: the first was the attempt to buy a liberal democracy; the second is an attempt to buy a revolution.[12] Both systems are ersatz.

After many years of running seemingly well on oil money, the Venezuelan two-party system collapsed when the money ran out, and was replaced by a single leader who has concentrated power and remains popular thanks to a bond with many Venezuelans reinforced by quantities of new oil revenues for social programs. The change was baptized a "Bolivarian revolution," and the new society "twenty-first century socialism."[13]

The stages of Chávez's construction of power and consent were clear and distinct, and fuelled by oil. First—after his election as president— the launching of a referendum to form a constituent assembly, not only as a means to create a new institutional framework, but also to check a Congress where the *chavistas* were a minority. This was the "Gaullist" phase. Next, having attained that goal, between 2000 and 2002 Chávez acted internally and internationally to provoke a rise in the price of oil and at the same time gain control of PDVSA, the state oil company. This was the "Nasserist" phase. The third period, between 2002 and 2004, saw an even greater control of the economy in which a system of redistribution of resources and the organization of consensus was created. This also entailed the development of a *chavista* base in popular groups that transcended the previous organizational structures and political allegiances of the power coalition. This was the "Peronist" phase. Last, since 2005 Chávez entered a fourth phase, that of the construction of socialism with greater similarities to the Cuban system of control.[14] Venezuelans may have enthroned a president for life, in symbiosis with Cuba, with a political life expectancy determined by the avatars of energy markets.[15]

A democracy that is not buttressed by independent institutions, such as an efficient civil service, a proper judiciary, a legislature that is more than a rubber stamp for the executive, and a market economy where people learn the values of initiative, compromise, and trust is only a democracy by half. As an economic system, the overextended and intrusive state instead of organizing markets disorganizes production. Ritual elections in the absence of this institutional "software" neither advance true democracy nor sustain development.

Venezuela has turned its back on the harder-to-follow good recipe: construct both pillars of democracy at the same time—popular participation with social justice on the one hand, and independent political and economic institutions on the other. Only then will oil revenues be put to good use and the cycle of dependency can be broken.

In Latin America as a whole, the present crisis will break old ties, split elites, and produce severe social pressures. But at the same time it will weaken old and stubborn obstacles to change. A lot will depend on the shrewdness and foresight of those in power. Neither populism nor nationalism nor anti-imperialism offer viable courses: they are no more than fleeting celebrations that quickly turn sour. Prudent policies for independent development are far less flashy. They are based on long-term vision, serious regional collaboration, and a broad consensus regarding state policy. Countries such as Chile and Brazil are already headed down this wise path.

In a previous chapter I explored the possibilities for development contained in ongoing geopolitical shifts. Old modes of trade and financial dependence have been replaced by new patterns of exports and growth. This prompted the coining of the phrase "Chimericas." An understanding of the pros and cons of dependency theory leads us in this case to sound a note of warning and to anticipate future crisis. From this perspective, the main danger is the repetition—in the relationship with China—of classic patterns of dependency of one hundred years ago, when the tendency was for the terms of trade between primary and manufactured goods to deteriorate. In those days, economic power accrued for the technologically advanced. Today China is a major market for Latin American commodities. But Asia and Latin America have different models of integrating into the world economy. Latin America does not rely on a steady government hand to guide its way into global markets. China does. In that context, markets have decided that China's growth is partly fuelled by primary commodities and raw materials from Latin America, and that Chinese products are more attractive in the high technology markets of the world. If this trend continues, Latin America will fall vis-à-vis China into an old pattern of dependency.[16] A study conducted by Kevin P. Gallagher and Roberto Porzecanski from Tufts University's Global Development and Environment Institute indicates that Latin America is falling behind when it comes to penetrating high technology export markets, and is losing ground to China.[17] If markets decide that Latin America's exchange rates are overvalued, the region can face a serious crisis. Only conscious and steady policies that favor the technical development of agribusiness, and a policy of industrial and high value-added diversification can prevent a fall into the old dependency trap.

There is much that is useful and salvageable from dependency theory, and other theories of the past (including Minsky's and Keynes's) provided that the policy errors of the past are avoided. There is no better time than the present crisis to dust off some old theories, draw from them what is valuable, and disregard what is obsolete. This exercise will help us determine which ties have been severed in the current crisis and which new ties need to be formed in the financial and productive order and, above all, what type of regional integration is viable and desirable.

Chapter Eight

LATIN AMERICA IN THE WORLD
OF LATE CAPITALISM

As we have seen, global capitalism is in crisis and each region does its best to wiggle within it. The diagnosis and the proposals multiply. It is important to take stock of the different views and ask: What is Latin America's destiny in this new world?

The recent publication of William I. Robinson's *Latin America and Global Capitalism: A Critical Globalization Perspective*[1] that tries to think "outside the box" about the predicament and the options for Latin America allows me to survey the field of interpretations of the world crisis and the region's position within it. This volume is part of a welcome turn to the classic roots of political economy. In it "globalization" refers to the dynamics of late capitalism, an economic system that now covers the entire planet and "critical" means that the system must be examined in terms of costs and benefits, potentiality and actuality.

Taking Positions

The field of globalization studies is organized around a set of questions about late capitalism and its various articulations in different areas—in this case Latin America.[2] The situation of the field has been well stated by Eric Hobsbawm, who maintains that the paradigm capitalism/socialism is over.[3] Moreover, the failure of socialism preceded the bankruptcy of capitalism. In fact, the socialist collapse may have precipitated the current capitalist crisis by launching an unopposed search for cheap labor—with the consequent migration of industry to hitherto out-of-bounds nations—and the overspecialization of former industrial countries in the service sector, including financial speculation and leveraged consumption. We are now witnessing the rebalancing of that unsustainable dynamic.

The situation presents a paradox for radicals, for whom socialism would ultimately succeed capitalism. Such outcome is unlikely. Neo-Marxists hope that the present crisis of world capitalism will usher in a new wave of revolutionary movements. In such view, a new "march towards socialism" is happening in various parts of Latin America and will become a source of international inspiration. Some parts of the diagnosis ring true—but on the whole it is a pipe dream.

In the analysis of capitalist globalization and its crisis, interpretations from the right quadrant are lacking. Market fundamentalists have remained silent since the crisis started. The few exceptions are to be found in some newsletters circulated by investor gurus.

By and large, the economic establishment has moved to the left. The narrative is as follows. The crisis began in the American real estate market. It rapidly spread over the global financial system largely due to complex debt instruments that mixed good and bad assets and diluted financial responsibility. The system as a whole became opaque. The calculus of risk broke down.

The theoretical basis for this analysis can be found in the work of post-Keynesians for whom monetary systems tend towards financial instability, and produce speculative bubbles. The ensuing disorder requires the intervention of the public sector and the reform of financial institutions. In this view financial crises are recurrent and severe but not terminal. The debate centers on the scope of public intervention. Regardless of disagreements as to procedures and velocities, most economists concur in recognizing a need for a massive state intervention to reactivate credit, production, and demand.

Further to the left in the field of positions,[4] critics seem to be more in disagreement among themselves than mainline analysts. Some of them come close to the Keynesian school of thought and point to the financialization of the economy as the main source of the crisis. Some even go back to Marxist sources for the study of finance capital. Others follow the theses about "overproduction" and "under consumption." The thesis of the "unmanageable surplus" was once popular in the United States in the radical sixties. Likewise today, the great recession would be an expression of the "falling rate of profit."

Finally, postmodern theorists break the productivist mold of conventional analyses and point to what, in economic parlance, we may call the "internalization of externalities"—ranging from overpopulation to climate change—as the underlying force beneath the crisis. For them, capitalist society solves some of its problems at the cost of generating even bigger ones.[5]

Various geopolitical interpretations follow closely the theoretical positions. Some see new capitalist powers emerging to challenge older hegemons, with the ensuing risk of war. Others see instead a less traumatic "passing of the baton" from the West to the East. Others yet envisage new ruling alliances, such as a reformed G-20, a rising G-2, or an evolving Chimerica. And there are those who sense the dawn of a world order in which a major shift will take place towards public action, prodded by a looming environmental catastrophe.

The calls for action are also varied. Some propose a radicalized set of Keynesian policies to tame capitalism. Others believe that socialism has found its second wind, and there are those who think modernity itself will be replaced by a different type of civilization.

Where do "critical globalization studies" fit in this field of positions and proposals? In my view: somewhere between Marxism and postmodern anti-globalism as abridged above. In their interpretation of global capitalism and in their treatment of Latin America, critical anti-globalists tend to overgeneralize. They give short shrift to the varieties of capitalism—a subject with a rich scholarship. Likewise, they gloss over the striking diversity of national experiences, at a time when most experts refuse to define a single Latin American problematique, as was done earlier around concepts such as "development," "revolution," "dependency," "modernization," and "democratization." They seem to uphold the notion that a single paradigm of causal relationships exists.

Disclaimers notwithstanding, anti-globalists are resolute determinists. The concepts of expanded reproduction, commoditization, phases of accumulation, and stages of development they use are culled from standard Marxism. Their own contribution is to bring the analysis forward in time.

The grand narrative is familiar: capitalism is driven by underlying "laws of motion" which lead to periodic crises, at which points the ruling elites redesign the system for further bouts of growth. Critics dwell especially on the last experiment in capitalist redesign, neoliberalism, which they portray in Spenglerian tones. Here Marxist materialism lapses into idealism. Neoliberalism becomes a *Zeitgeist* that wreaks havoc on the planet. With the exception of Cuba, all regimes in the region—military and civilian alike—were presumably streamlined to the requirements of transnational companies and elites.

The account—quite popular in Latin American progressive circles—is too much of a gloss. The methodological problem has been described as a "historical Doppler effect,"[6] which—similar to acoustics—creates a more homogeneous interpretation for distant eras and sharper, more complex interpretations in periods closer to the present. The Doppler effect leads to the logical fallacy of *post hoc ergo propter hoc*—the illusion that what has happened necessarily had to happen, when in fact, upon closer examination, all action faces algorithmic forks. The most interesting research on Latin America separates the political, social, and economic processes, and maps their combinations in variable matrices without assuming a single line of causation.[7]

Neo-Marxism modulates its determinism of course. In the past, it sees actors as agents of structure; in the present, as a counterpoint of domination and resistance. In the future, it sees a number of conflicts and mobilizations—ranging from indigenous Andean movements to the struggles of unemployed blue-collar workers in greater Buenos Aires—coming together under a Single Social Movement that would supersede capitalism. Diversity is reduced to unity, and disparate historical trajectories are boiled down to an all-or-nothing option—as in the old slogan *socialisme ou barbarie*.

I beg to disagree. The past is less over-determined and the future less dire. Latin America will continue to consume more history than it can produce. As during the Great Depression, the response in the region is pragmatic and sometimes innovative, but not world-shaking. Brazil, the largest country in the area and the one with a sizeable emerging middle class, will surge ahead and become a player on the great international chessboard. Its challenge will be the reduction of inequality. Mexico, on the other hand, will reboot development on the coattails of an American recovery. It will continue to be too close to the US for comfort. Argentina, as always, will muddle through more thanks to the bounty of nature than to the wisdom of its leadership. Chile will continue on its path of steady growth and good governance, with closer links to the Asia-Pacific region than to its immediate neighborhood. The Andean countries will pursue the inclusion of the long-marginalized native majorities, but without any significant spillover to the rest of the continent. Only Venezuela will follow a path to "twenty-first century socialism." The question here is: will the Bolivarian revolution succumb to the natural resource curse and a self-destructive dynamic? This sample illustrates the diversity of experiences. Just as neoliberalism has had different interpretations, so will the roads out of the world crisis differ from each other. Like the River Plate, continental solidarity is wide but also shallow.

In this diverse panorama there is one heartening fact: as opposed to other regions of the world, inequality is diminishing in Latin America. The causes are varied. The rise of conditional cash transfer programs, such as Brazil's *Bolsa Família*, a monthly income supplement of up to $75, subject to school attendance, paid to 11 million families is one cause. Some 17 countries in Latin America, covering 70 million beneficiaries, run similar schemes. Second, inequality fell due to better primary and secondary education coverage. This led to a greater supply of skilled workers and eroded the premium that skilled labor first enjoyed when trade was liberalized in the 1980s. Unskilled labor meanwhile commanded pay increases as it was in relative short supply.[11] All this is good news. Sadly, it is only a first step down a long road. Even at the recent impressive rates of decline in inequality, it will take Brazil another two decades before they fall to average world levels. And the easy wins from cash transfer schemes may soon be over. For inequality to fall further, there is a need for upgrades, for example in the quality of primary and secondary education. Large investments in the upgrading of human capital and infrastructure are essential. The challenge of inclusion under capitalist growth requires bold public endeavors.

Neo-Marxists propose a different view, hostile to free markets. Not only is Venezuela's revolution seen as sustainable but also as a superior model—thanks to dialectic of permanent popular mobilization. These critics acknowledge the many inconsistencies of the Bolivarian transformation but think they can be overcome. The fact is that oil wealth, under socialism or not, has corrupted Venezuela as a trust fund can corrupt a child. Democratic politicians fed a fantasy of quick wealth for decades, and now Chávez is doing it too. The country is run as a reality television show. Maladministration is rampant. The state-oil company has become the center of an arbitrary command economy that does not function well. The few state functions that work reasonably well are the intelligence service and Cuba's social missions that deliver basic health care to Venezuela's poor—few carrots and a robust stick. Yet why call this process "twenty-first century socialism" and not "plebiscitary leader democracy" (following Max Weber), which involves charisma, cumulative radicalization— and regime collapse? To think that the experiment can be replicated in places like Brazil, Mexico, Argentina, or Chile is a fantasy. Much as these critics castigate those who propose a distinction between a "well-behaved" and a "bad" left in Latin America,[9] they propose a similar Manichean dichotomy between a reformist and a revolutionary left.

Sometimes such analyses manage to pour new wine in old bottles. The neo-Marxist perspective contains an alternative, albeit controversial, view of new globalization processes in Latin America, such as a consideration of industrial subcontracting, transnational services, tourism, the export of labor, and migration, and highlights important data on ongoing social processes.

The radical grand finale, on the other hand, places unwarranted hopes on a single continent that will shine upon the world the light of a brighter future. To skeptics like myself, Latin America is an area of pragmatic experimentation. To contemporary anti-globalists and lingering enthusiasts of third-world revolutions it is a projective Eden that will redeem their disappointments with history.

Chapter Nine

A GARDEN OF FORKING PATHS

The crisis at the core of the global economy, and especially the ensuing absence of imagination, the hesitation, and the insufficiency of the response among leaders have caused perplexity among Latin Americans. The crisis has not been catastrophic in the South of the globe. It has left many countries with more freedom from the North, but that also means with fewer excuses to avoid self-examination. More freedom yes, but freedom to do what? I subscribe to the notion that capitalism is fate, but that is not a consolation, because its own future is uncertain. We are creatures of a world historical process that has no return, yet it has led us to hard choices. How to reconcile the indispensability of a system with policies that avert its most pernicious consequences? Capitalism teeters on the verge of bankruptcy; the tried alternatives to it have been wanting—if not outright unviable or worse. What therefore is to be done? Latin America is a region of bewildering diversity, so its visions, and its reactions to the world crisis also vary. My task in this chapter is to highlight the differences, but also to point to common themes. Here are some of the dilemmas, beginning with the overall system and zooming in on the different trajectories of some countries enmeshed in its web.

In classical sociology, ever since the work of Max Weber, modern capitalism has been understood both as an economic system and as a socio-cultural complex whose origins were unusual but whose destiny was global. This admixture of contingency and necessity, of the unique and the general, shaped in Weber's view our "fate." Insofar as capitalism is as much a cultural as an economic system, the formal economic models of its functioning fail on one important score: they ignore the messiness of social relations and the roots of economic behavior in habits and institutions—what sociologists refer to as "path dependency."

Following in the footsteps of Max Weber, the historian Joyce Appleby, in a recent study,[1] insists that far from being inevitable, the advent of capitalism was "a startling departure from the norms that had prevailed for four thousand years." Once broken however, those ancient norms did not return. In short, for Weber and for Appleby, capitalism opened in history a one-way street.

Once established, capitalism is "poised to crush any opposition to its expansion."

The advent in the twentieth century of anti-capitalist systems did not entail a restitution of the pre-capitalist norms. Just as capitalism required in its day a radical reconception of human nature,[2] so did socialism require an equivalent shift. With the benefit of hindsight in the twenty-first century we can state that whereas the capitalist reconception of human nature "took," the socialist effort did not. Socialism was the attempt to move beyond the partial rationality of capitalism—the persistent but anarchic pursuit of productivity—toward a total rationality that would dispense of private property, of the search for gain, and of market signals, either incrementally or in one broad sweep.

Perhaps the most salient motivation of this quest for complete rationality is the abolition of inequality. This quest has old roots not in traditional norms but in more subterranean and antinomian streams—that is why it can mobilize in the same amalgam of utopian hopes and obscure memories, from the Levelers and the Diggers in the English revolution to Gracchus Babeuf in the French. Although I cannot develop the argument in the narrow confines of this book, I believe that socialism is less about the abolition of poverty than about the abolition of difference. In this particular sense then, the twentieth century can be interpreted as an asymmetrical contest between socialism's quest for equality and capitalism's quest for prosperity.

As stated in previous chapters, the predicament of the twenty-first century on such registry can be formulated thus: socialism failed, and capitalism, which "won," is now in serious crisis. But the failure of one and the crisis of the other should not daunt us if we see them as problems only of their "pure types." The time seems ripe for abandoning the twentieth-century paradigm of either-or, and for exploring instead a variety of modular admixtures suitable to a variety of contexts, North and South, East and West. The policy implications of this pragmatic—as opposed to dogmatic—view are momentous.

Running through the great variety of experiences in the continent is a deep and constant theme: How to grow sustainably and hence attain prosperity without leaving people behind? In this chapter I have chosen four Latin American countries to show the interplay between equality and prosperity—what is gained and what is lost when accenting one social value or the other. The four are different in culture, languages, developmental paths, and ethnic composition. Two countries—Mexico and Brazil—represent, in different ways, the promise and the difficulties of globalized capitalism as a remedy for easing poverty. (I could have chosen just as well Chile and Uruguay.) The accent on prosperity here is key. The other two countries—Cuba and Argentina—represent, also in very different manners, the dilemmas and the price of instituting equality. (I could have chosen Bolivia and Venezuela too.) The accent on social justice here is key.

Cuba's Dead End

From Hope to Fear: The Dilemma of Radical Equality

Ten years after the triumph of the Chinese revolution, in the Americas the island of Cuba underwent an equivalent upheaval. The Cuban revolution provoked an extraordinary interest and enthusiasm at the time throughout the world. In the middle of the Cold War, Cuba acquired a geopolitical significance out of proportion to its size and economic weight—and almost provoked a nuclear exchange between the two superpowers.

The importance of Cuba however, was of a different kind. The Cuban revolution was seen as the latest of a series of socialist experiments in moving beyond capitalism and towards a new society of radical equality. One could argue that Cuba closed an even longer cycle of revolutions.[3] In fact, the Cuban revolution vowed to "build a new man" and demanded nothing less than the reconception of human nature. The prestige and the lasting legitimacy of the Cuban revolution rested primarily on the equalization of social conditions and on the universal access to health and education—two achievements attained with record speed during the first decade of the revolution.

Those of us who were young in 1960 remember the passionate curiosity that the Cuban experiment provoked. That was in the West, where postwar prosperity had given rise to leftist libertarian hopes among the youth. In the communist East, where socialism had been imposed from above and from outside, and had solidified into an oppressive form of bureaucratic domination, the Cuban revolution seemed to offer a better hope. The following are recollections from a Romanian student: "Castro's energetic and long speeches, while visiting Romania, were listened to in people's houses with an admiration and a form of exotic respect that the Romanian dictator Ceaușescu never enjoyed. 'It's Fidel!'—old people were saying to me in a tone that resembled a mythological invocation. [...] Fidel seemed to have accomplished, in Romanian popular view at the time, something that local communism either failed to achieve or lost as a cause on its way."[4]

From a sociological and comparative point of view however, one must pose two different and perhaps disturbing questions: one, to what extent are those achievements linked to the totalitarian form of the regime that took shape during the initial surge of the revolution?; and two, what price did the Cuban society and economy pay for the relentless pursuit of total and egalitarian inclusion? In other words, is there an inner logic that connects the enforcement of social justice with the absence of civic and public rights, with police repression, and with the prohibition to emigrate? The official complaints in the capitalist West about the violation of human rights fail to fathom a completely different view of what is right and what is wrong, a view of the world that does not recognize as legitimate any act of dissent or abstention, or the embrace of difference—in Albert Hirschman's words, that refuses to consider voice and exit as worthy of respect.[5]

In a recent and courageous book on Cuba, Claudia Hilb addresses these two questions.[6] She approaches them historically, and chronicles the intimate association between two processes during the first decade of the revolution, namely, the rapid equalization of conditions imposed by the revolutionary regime upon the entire society and the extraordinary concentration of power in the figure of Fidel Castro. According to this author, the one makes no sense without the other. The entire revolutionary project was one of transforming society from the top—in Foucault's terms, from a high point of total visibility, surveillance, and control. According to this analysis, the revolution was panoptical from the beginning. The project rode on a wave of popular enthusiasm and a collective feeling of emancipation from a corrupt and despotic past. It was not therefore the voluntary or unwitting replacement of one despotism for another, but something very different: a radical overhaul of existing inequalities that required total and central control *and* mass participation.

In Max Weber's typology of the forms of legitimation, the revolution joined together rational (in the sense of systematic and meticulous control) and charismatic domination. This coincidence of the rational and the charismatic is a phase through which most revolutions pass. In the long run however, rationality trumps the "cult of personality," and true to Weber's prediction, charisma becomes bureaucratically "routinized." The Cuban peculiarity consists in the persistence of charisma and the longevity of Fidel—a process that has provided the regime with long-range stability but ultimate fragility. Aside from these distinctions, what count for the present discussion are the speed, the depth, and the manner of construction of an egalitarian society during the first phase of the revolution.

In a very abridged form, what one discerns in this period is the rapid equalization of society from the bottom up, by favoring the rise of the downtrodden and the excluded, but enforced 'without ifs or buts' from the top of political power. In Hilb's view, radical equalization and centralization of control were two sides of the same coin, two constitutive elements of the same process.

The first ten years witnessed two agrarian reforms: the first an expropriation, break-up, and redistribution of large holdings to the landless, and the second an imposition of state control over all agricultural production, large and small. The non-agrarian sectors of the economy, too, were nationalized and passed into the property of the state: foreign subsidiaries, sugar refineries, commerce, utilities, and construction. The state also took control of health and education, and regulated housing. All these measures favored those at the bottom of the social pyramid, and progressively alienated those above, first the privileged elite and then the middle class, including small property owners initially favored by redistribution. Each wave of equalization produced a corresponding wave of exile—first the recalcitrant, then the disenchanted. In the words of Barrington Moore Jr., in reference to a similar but much more severe process in the early phases of the Soviet revolution,[7] this was a period of "terror and progress." Popular mobilization went hand in hand with severe repression.

At the top level of leadership a voluntaristic model of forced development prevailed (first embodied in the figure of Ernesto 'Che' Guevara and subsequently by Fidel Castro himself), with the stress on altruistic as opposed to material incentives. In the language of the times, it was an attempt to construct socialism (efforts-based compensation) and communism (needs-based compensation) simultaneously. In practical terms, the process eliminated all the economic agents that were not agents of the state.

What was the upshot? At the sociological level, there was a radical leveling of difference and distinction; at the economic level, a phenomenal disorganization of production. The economic dislocation happened in part due to the eviction and exodus of qualified strata, but more significantly due to the inability of the state to manage and to allocate activities without market signals. The former was a serious but temporary effect, the latter a fatal flaw.

The centralization of control in the hands of one person and the repression or marginalization of any other center of decision-making affected not only the "natural" enemies of the revolution, but its original supporters as well. The control and "coordination" of student organizations, of labor unions, and finally of the cultural and artistic producers, has been well documented by analysts throughout the years and is also available in the form of recollections and memoirs. A similar process occurred with the single party of the revolution, which through successive purges became a docile communist machine, subordinated to Fidel. As in other soviet-type regimes, those "in the cockpit" were in constant fear of "falling out of grace."

For the wider society, quieter forms of what Russian sociologist Victor Zaslavsky called "organized consensus" gradually replaced the initial enthusiasm of revolutionary mobilization.[8] A vast network of surveillance and thought control was established through the committees for the defense of the revolution, police informants, and the active encouragement of denunciations of acquaintances, relatives, and friends. Daily life under such conditions passed from a state of charismatic endorsement to a culture of fear, perhaps best illustrated by the German film *The Lives of Others*,[9] which portrays the social psychology of control in the former DDR (Deutsche Demokratische Republik, or East Germany)—the epitome of soviet-style societies. The result was the corrosion of civil forms of conviviality, which have been studied in other contexts as well.[10] From an economic point of view, it meant the downgrading of initiative and morale, which reinforced the incompetence of the state and required ever more unpleasant dispositions, like *desabastecimiento* (stock outs) and rationing.

If on the political level the regime survived through repression, on the macroeconomic level it was on the dole of the former Soviet Union. When the latter collapsed, Cuba suffered enormous penury until it was partially bailed out by the help of Chávez's oil-rich Venezuela. The early dependence on the USSR tempered the initial voluntarism of the revolution,[11] and the aggressive but clumsy foreign policy of the United States helped to provide a justification for tightening control. But ultimately the model of soviet-type society that was established in Cuba was the product of a deep internal logic.

Forced equality produced economic disincentives and dysfunctions negatively affecting growth and prosperity—among them ersatz full employment, absenteeism, theft of public property, a clandestine market, and a "double morality" of conformity and deviance. For example, an ordinary Cuban would ritually denounce the exiles in Miami but cash in on remittances by relatives in the United States. Moreover, the regime soon discovered that social inequality has not one source but many—and that the regime was generating its own. For as Charles Tilly has shown, inequality is not a mere gradient susceptible of measurement along one dimension (as for instance with the Gini coefficient), but a series of categorical distinctions based on different means and resources.[12]

The Autumn of the Patriarch

As time goes by and the original leadership faces old age and death, Cuba teeters unprepared for a transition to a world that, although mired in crisis, no longer accepts the mode of life that Cubans have withstood during a heavy fifty years. Excluding inequality, on many other comparative indicators, Cuba today does not fare better than it did in 1959. Comparing it to poorer Caribbean nations will not do—the comparison is with Chile, Uruguay, or Brazil. Today, as then, the relative position is pretty much the same. The conclusion is sobering: Cuba has attained greater social equality at the price of political repression and economic stagnation. It lives in a bubble of silence and denial, as in a museum of a way of life that nobody wants.[13] Over the past fifty years, the revolution has spent the moral capital reserves it held as a bastion of dignified resistance to the colossus of the North. The question pending for the future is how to accede to a modality of economic growth that does not destroy the social achievements of the past—how to throw out the communist bathwater without ejecting the egalitarian baby as well.[11] That is a tall order indeed.

The world of late capitalism does offer examples of managed transitions from egalitarian socialism to an unequal but prosperous market society—some more attractive than others.[15] In some intellectual and policy circles there is discussion of the "Vietnamese way" in which the communist power structure itself sponsors an opening of the country to capitalist investment, while protecting not just its own interests but also social solidarity. A superficial overview of social behavior however, raises the question of whether the Cubans—after decades of forced-fed altruism—have not lost their appetite for solidarity as well as the initiative for entrepreneurship that East Asians managed to retain. Travelers from Brazil to Cuba these days report that, although the two populations live in the tropics, Brazilians exude and exalt life, but Cubans seem numb.

If the Cuban leadership decided to undertake "Vietnamese reforms" the situation would look like this. The regime would propose measures that would give greater scope to the private sector, reduce the budget deficit, and boost the output of agricultural and consumer goods in order to raise market supplies and exports. Specifically, the government would seek to make prices more responsive to market forces and to allow farmers and industrial producers to make profits. Barriers to trade would be lowered; the checkpoint inspection system that requires goods in transit to be frequently inspected would be abolished; and regulations on private inflow of money, goods, and tourists from overseas would be relaxed. In the state-controlled industrial sector, overstaffing in state administrative and service organizations would be slated for reduction. Government leaders also would plan to restructure the tax system to boost revenue and improve incentives. Nontraditional exports would increase, while outside investors would regain their faith. As in Vietnam, the economy would then grow at 6 per cent or more a year, inequality would increase (an inevitable byproduct of a capitalist surge), but poverty would diminish significantly. With luck and investments from another tropical republic—Brazil—Cuba could mitigate its dependence on foreign fossil fuels and become a net exporter of sugar ethanol. The transition would mean for Cuba another large social experiment, this time based no longer exclusively on the socialist proposition that austerity and sacrifice should be shared equally, but also on the capitalist proposition that a rising tide lifts all boats.

In the immediate future, Cuba will navigate treacherous waters—a passage full of danger between the Scylla and Charybdis of two rent-seeking mafias, one inside the country and the other one outside:[16] on the one hand the attempt by exiles to settle accounts, and on the other the pretensions of functionaries of the regime to become the new capitalist masters, Russian style.[17]

More than fifty years ago, a young rebellious student called Fidel Castro led a failed assault on the fortress of Moncada. He was arrested and tried. In his defense, he gave a speech that became famous, "History will absolve me." For the next fifty years history was kind to him because he made it, wrote it, and kept it under firm control. The other History to which he referred in his youthful speech could not possibly absolve him—because it does not exist. What remains of its ghost is a question mark in the sky, under which Fidel and his system wither dismally with age.

Brazil's Path Ahead

A Giant in Search of Autonomy and Prosperity

During the twentieth century, by most common indicators Brazil counted as one of the most unequal societies in the world. In geopolitical terms it supplied troops for Western allies in world conflicts but did not count as a heavy weight. In its own vicinity, and despite the occasional energy provided by traditional rivalries with Argentina, other Latin Americans considered Brazil as *un gigante dormido* (a sleeping giant). In many ways Brazil was an anomaly. Its ethnic mix, its language, its historical trajectory, its popular culture, and its sheer size set the country aside from the Latin American rest.

One could argue that it is easier to compare Brazil to the United States than to Colombia or Peru. Although usually unacknowledged, the comparison with the US holds on several counts. The two countries are of almost identical size, with very large populations (the US is larger by one third); both were founded on a double stream of European settlers and African slaves; today they are both multiethnic; and curiously, each country has the highest rate of social inequality of its type—the US in the developed world, and Brazil in the developing world. Despite this cleavage, both Brazilians and Americans are can-do nations of pilgrims, searchers, and dreamers—believers in boundless possibility, from their respective presidents on down.[18] Brazil did not have a Tocqueville to take its pulse early on, but it deserved one. "Democracy in Brazil" would have then rivaled *Democracy in America* as a portrait of early democratic experimentalism. Never mind that the US was a republic, and Brazil an empire (the only country in the Americas that instead of declaring independence from the metropolis, *imported* it wholesale). True, Americans forged early their own institutions, which happened to work, and which they hold in reverent respect since the early days of the republic. Brazilians, on the other hand imported theirs, and never truly believed in them.

At the end of the twentieth century and especially since the beginning of the twenty-first, the giant awoke. Brazil found its stride. With the consolidation of democracy and sound macroeconomic policies, Brazil became confident in its future and prepared to face most storms. When the world financial crisis broke out, Brazilian authorities were calm and collected. The doom and gloom in many countries did not infect Brazil, where President Luiz Inácio Lula da Silva showed unprecedented self-assurance. Speaking in Madrid in the middle of the crisis, Lula said that "this idea that markets can do everything is over," and more fundamentally, "The times in which emerging countries depended on the IMF are over." This was not Hugo Chávez speaking, but the president of Latin America's largest economy, who enjoyed 80 per cent popularity in his country. Lula also alluded to the fact that Basel rules had been applied to banks in Brazil but not in the US. "That has to end," he said. Since 1995, banks in Brazil had complied with an 11 per cent capital requirement—one of the highest in Latin America—and Lula wanted new regulations of the world financial markets that would be stricter on banks from advanced countries.

Such a high level of confidence about Brazil's economy reflected some underlying economic fundamentals that have helped Brazil to manage the crisis: foreign reserves were $205 billion, four times higher than in 2004; primarily domestic institutions—though low for developed country standards—conducted financial intermediation; and foreign-owned bank assets came to only 30 per cent, compared to over 80 per cent in Mexico. To the extent that Brazilian banks also had very low foreign liabilities, the economy was somewhat protected from a major credit contraction in international financial markets. Looking at these fundamentals of the Brazilian economy, there were good reasons therefore to believe that Brazil's economy would be resilient to the global financial crisis. That does not mean that Brazil is immune, but Brazil could cope, and it has coped.

For two decades now, first under the two Cardoso presidencies, and at an accelerated pace with Lula's two administrations, Brazil has embarked on the search—if not yet the full practice—of a model of development that while embracing capitalism, uses capitalist tools to broaden opportunities to a rising middle class. In many ways, the project has an elective affinity with an old American experiment, in greatest evidence in the North during most of the nineteenth and of the twentieth centuries—from early homesteading by small and medium farmers in the days of the frontier to the massive growth of a productive and consuming middle class after the Second World War.

In the US then, as with Brazil now, it was not all bread and roses, but there was real progress for the common man and woman, before, during, and after industrialization. Prosperity trumped equality at every turn, but the unequal distribution of wealth was kept within reasonable bounds, tempered by the rising wealth of the nation. Over the last few decades however, the concentration of income, the financialization of the economy, and the transfer of the industrial platform abroad have led to a social regression,[19] disguised in various ways. American common women and men have experienced a significant reduction of real income and a shrinking share of the national wealth. Surveys indicate for the first time a rising skepticism about the prospects of intergenerational mobility.

Brazil, on the other hand, seems to have found its pace and quickened the rhythm of growth in many sectors of the economy: agriculture, industry, energy, mineral extraction, and services. Brazilian elites have learned to distinguish between government and state, between the politics of the moment and the larger interests of the long run. They are not afraid of market reforms. The old middle classes in Brazil do feel the status decline and compression of prospects of their American (or Argentinean) counterparts. But other millions of Brazilians have recently moved up the social ladder. These persons are full of energy and hope, ready to undertake new production in thousands of small and medium enterprises. Whereas in America the loss of jobs is leading to reactionary populism, in Brazil the new middle class offers a vast space for democratic experimentalism. It has become the social base of progressive capitalism.[20] In American English, the expression "has gone south" denotes a business deal that went sour and failed. It has a negative connotation. In the world of late capitalism however, "going south," means something else: the transfer of economic energy and of the hopes for prosperity to a different place.

As Brazil has moved from—in the language of Fernando Henrique Cardoso—"dependent development" to a more autonomous status as master of its house, so has its foreign policy become more assertive and independent. Since the beginning of the twentieth century, Brazil's ambition has been to see its natural role as a big country recognized in the international arena. The idea of Brazil's eventual emergence as a great power was always present in the mind of Brazilian elites but was thwarted until now—at last it has the tools and resources to realize its vision. The old Brazilian ambitions to play an increasingly autonomous role in the world and, eventually, to conquer a prominent place in the international system, seem finally within reach in the new millennium. The two principles of autonomy and universality now shape its relationship with the United States and with the other Latin American countries.

During the Cold War, Brazilian elites considered the bipolar international order an obstacle to its country's strategic goals. For this reason Brazilian diplomacy (usually identified with Itamaraty, its Rio's headquarters) had pursued a strategy defined as "autonomy through distance," which consisted of the refusal to accept the consolidation of international institutions that would legitimize and perpetuate the existing world order.

With the fall of the Berlin Wall, Brazil saw an opportunity to participate more fully in the shaping of a new world order, and changed its strategy from a defensive to a proactive one. The new strategy entailed greater attention to the region, starting with closer ties with its traditional Southern rival, Argentina, and leading to regional integration through Mercosur (*Mercado Común del Sur,* or *Southern Common Market,* a Regional Trade Agreement among Argentina, Brazil, Paraguay and Uruguay founded in 1991). The succession of President Cardoso with President Lula marked a further evolution of foreign policy, with an even stronger emphasis on autonomy, and with a greater focus on the South-South cooperation with China, India, and South Africa, while relations with the other Latin American countries were put on the back burner. The pursuit of greater standing among world powers had priority over the pursuit of regional integration. With the advent of the world crisis and the perceived decline of American power, new opportunities have opened for Brazil and its ambitions.

Brazil and the United States

In contrast to Mexico, Brazil has always felt closer to God than to the United States. Traditionally the relations between the US and Brazil have oscillated between relaxed and tense, but never reaching the level of open hostility that occasionally erupted in other parts of the continent. There was however, an asymmetry, which Brazilians resented. After WWII Brazil was not very relevant to US foreign policy, even during the Cold War when Latin America was paramount to US interests. Brazil's importance decreased even further after the collapse of the Soviet Union, as Washington was left as the only superpower on the scene. The Bush and Clinton administrations tried to tie Latin America officially to the US sphere of influence, first with the creation of NAFTA (North American Free Trade Association) and then with a plan (aborted) for a continental area of free trade. The attacks of 9/11 pushed Latin America further down the list of priorities on the American agenda.

For Brazil, on the contrary, relations with the US were always crucial because of the sheer fact of American power—even though economically Brazil was no longer dependent (as it was during the first half of the twentieth century) on the US market for its principal exports. Brazilian foreign policy was polite and accommodating, but chafed at the bit and waited for an opportunity to free itself from American constraints. Even at the height of the Cold War, Brazil tried, without much benefit or success, to partake of non-alignment.

The end of the Cold War opened the first big opportunity to diversify Brazilian interests and relations with other blocs and with the emerging markets. This move—a veritable strike for autonomy—was more successful than the attempt to lead the formation of a Latin American bloc. With its traditional preference for multilateralism, Brazil's activities in the world have tried to combine two goals: becoming a leading power, but at the same time promoting the idea of a more democratic globalization, to be achieved through the enhanced participation of populous countries traditionally excluded from decision making.

Brazil and the Americas

The very same forces that gave Brazil greater room to maneuver gave other countries in Latin America the chance to challenge the United States with their own, more radical proposals—and put Brazilian regional ambitions in abeyance. To date, Brazil has not been able to use its own version of regional integration as a lever to lift itself further in the world by becoming the spokesman for Latin America. Nevertheless, as opposed to the noisier postures of Argentina, Bolivia, or Venezuela (designed more for nuisance value than for a practical contribution to development), Brazil, like China, holds a strategic card of great significance: patience. For the moment, Brazil has a much bigger role in world affairs, though few followers in Latin America.[21]

During the 1970s and the 1980s, Brazil identified relations with other Latin American countries as a major foreign policy priority. In the perspective of the Brazilian elites, integration with Argentina and the rest of the Southern Cone would be very important. On the one hand, it would be a mechanism for trade liberalization. On the other, the bloc could become a platform for international bargaining, and a lever for Brazil to throw its weight in the international arena. From the Brazilian perspective, regional hegemony, through a consolidation of Mercosur would permit a better exercise of universalism and enhance the negotiating ability of the country. In theory that was correct, but in practice the project has faced two obstacles, one internal and the other external. Internally, integration carried a cost in reduced autonomy, and was seen by many Brazilians as a limiting factor on Brazil's dealing with the rest of the world. Externally, other countries, like Venezuela, have launched rival hegemonic projects of their own, effectively contesting the leadership of Brazil. The net result was that Latin American regional integration was stalled. Today it is at best a partial project and a distant goal.[22]

The Promise

Brazil is very unequal, but Brazil is hopeful, and it grows. The country has violent contrasts, and violent slums. *Eppur si muove* (and yet it indeed moves). In face of the world economic crisis, Brazilian elites consider insufficient the shallow responses in the North, and are amazed at the poverty of ideas in the very center of late capitalism.

As seen in other chapters, the American discussion—and to an extent the European one— has revolved around a mummified and shrunken version of Keynes. The three ideas that circulate are: how to rescue the financial sector? how to regulate the banks? and how far to extend the stimulus of monetary and fiscal policy? But, as Roberto Mangabeira Unger has argued, those ideas actually conceal and suppress three more important concerns worldwide. The first is the need to overcome the structural imbalance between the countries with huge deficits and the countries with huge surpluses, the savers and the dissavers. As I have tried to show before, this is the Achilles' heel of Chimerica. Second, behind the quest for regulation there is an urgent but unheeded need to reorganize the relationship between production and finance. The simplest question could bring down a house of cards: What is the purpose of all the money held in megabanks? In late capitalism, finance capital has been hegemonic but has a tenuous relation to the productive economy. The issue is all the more important since modern economic science has largely failed to understand the nature of finance. The policy question that follows is equally pressing: How to channel savings into long-term investments. Third and last, all countries must tackle in policy and in thought the linkage between recovery and redistribution, now that the violent concentration of wealth at the top, and the pseudo-democratization of credit at the bottom, have made the world economy hit a wall. In Latin America, those who favor a healthier kind of capitalism, from Hernando de Soto to Roberto Mangabeira,[23] have observed aghast how a property-owning democracy has been forfeited to a credit democracy in the first world, and they ask: is this a consummation of economic growth or its perversion?

If these are the real challenges behind the emergency and the first responses to it, the appropriate measures are easier to imagine—and perhaps also to implement—in some countries of the South than in many countries of the North. Brazil is a premier case in point. The measures are of three kinds. One is a set of strong countercyclical policies consisting of guarantees of a minimum wage, transfer measures, and public investment. Whereas in the US these measures have been partial and timid, in Brazil they could be bolder and enjoy wider social support. They would include an additional one: the lowering of the interest rate for targeted economic agents. Second, there should be a profound innovation in the institutions of a market economy, to magnify and sustain the effects of the first measures. They consist of investments in small and medium-sized enterprises, to jump start capitalism at the grass-root level. In Brazil, and in Latin America as a whole, this entails the introduction of a local system of finance—that is, the establishment of banks in the more backward regions. The third kind is a package of policies designed to quicken the pace of production in the penumbra of small undertakings at the bottom of the social pyramid, the productive mobilization of the poor who aspire to work and to learn.

From the heights of the state, it is not enough to institute enabling reforms for large market undertakings. It is even more important to support and enable those who work *sub rosa*, day and night, and those who form new self-help associations in the shadow of older and ineffectual institutions. The first, second, and third sectors of society, i.e. the state, private capital funds, and NGOs must direct no small resources to enhance what has already grown spontaneously—to make "democracy (productive, associational) work."[24]

The promise of Brazil consists of this: there is an enormous economic energy that seethes from below. It needs to be equipped with access to capital, technology, and world markets. It needs to be enabled with intelligent—and when necessary, "socialist"—educational and health policies. The world of late capitalism has grown us accustomed to the lure of rent at all social levels, high and low. That is decadent. There is a healthier path to wealth: the dynamo of socially inclusive growth. The proposal sounds utopian, but it is not: it consists not of dreaming what could be, but of energizing what already is.

Brazil has not wholeheartedly embarked upon this path yet, but the path is within reach. A choice not to take it would not halt Brazil's growth, but its prosperity would continue to be concentrated and its economy below potential, praying that Asian higher growth would pull it along and not stop. It is my belief that Brazil can take the lead of the BRICs, not just alphabetically.

Argentina's Decline

Social Justice and Squandered Plenty

Argentina is an outlier in the region and the globe. Because of it, the country has been the object of puzzlement and derision. Paul Samuelson used to quip that there were four types of countries in the world: developed, underdeveloped, Japan, and Argentina. Internationally, Argentina was the country in the Western Hemisphere that most frequently opposed American foreign policies apart from Cuba. This did not prevent Henry Kissinger from dismissing it as a "dagger pointed to the heart of Antarctica." In historical terms, I should add my own verdict: Argentina is a country underdeveloped through its own relentless efforts.

Argentine developmental patterns are unconventional indeed, for a number of reasons. Consider that Argentina was a rich country that went from wealth to bankruptcy over a period of about 70 years, between 1930 and 2001. Socially, it has always had the most developed middle class and the most educated population in Latin America, a region where strong middle classes and universal education are rare. Yet today, while a new and populous middle class is rising in Brazil, the Argentine middle class is in decline. Politically, Argentina saw the emergence and predominance of a unique movement: Peronism, which has survived for more than sixty years as a catchall party and the epitome of redistribution in the name of social justice. In sum, Argentina has been one of the most economically developed and one of the least politically stable countries in Latin America, a paradox that many of us have sought to explain, from Felix José Weill in the 1940s, to Guillermo O'Donnell in the 1970s, to my own description of a "fitful republic" in the 1980s.[25] In the end, political madness trumped development.

When I visit Argentina I hear stridently different voices. Those who support the government speak of a needed transfer of wealth from the rich to the poor, from the greedy landowners to the urban workers, of the valiant struggle against global capitalism, of progressive solidarity with Venezuela, Cuba, Bolivia, and Ecuador, of the right to repudiate the national debt, and of the right to confront the United States. Any opposition to this model is considered *destituyente* (de-stituent), in other words, subversive. Those in the opposition—a motley and bickering congregation—think of Argentina as a democracy that has been corrupted by the excessive concentration of power in the national executive, which governs bypassing any and all institutional checks and balances. What Argentina needs, they say, is a foundational agreement among all parties around a long-range strategy of development. But that is hard to envisage, since government and opposition consider each other as blameful and shameless.

Political passions of the moment aside, the predicament of Argentina is deep and of long date. The civic culture of the country, itself the result of accumulated frustrations and false starts, today shapes the quality of its politics. The impoverishment of the majority, which accelerated after the national default of 2001-2, makes it convenient for the political class—without distinction of parties—to gather votes by promising the redistribution of wealth in quick and dirty ways.

Politicians are not statesmen. They do not lead the country, but are led instead by the polls. The pursuit of their policies has deleterious effects, in turn, on any sustained development. In short, the distribution that they promise and that they enact creates disinvestment. It paradoxically maintains the situation that it purports to change. Argentine politics has become a management of its own dysfunctions. Social justice trumps prosperity, and the vicious circle is closed.

A different strategy would consist of attacking the root causes of poverty in the first place, not seeking to equalize it. It would mean, as is (partially) happening in Brazil, and has happened in Chile, enabling and equipping an independent middle class to work, to save, to invest, and to prosper. Civic responsibility stems from economic self-reliance, not from income transfers from the state. Then and only then can a virtuous circle begin. Only the destitute should be assisted. Everyone else should be empowered—even by the state when necessary—to succeed by themselves.

Whether in power or not, over many years Peronism has fostered among its followers and also among its rivals, a culture of protected, and often militant, mediocrity. That has been its legacy and hegemony. Such culture sponsors a model of development (heir to the import substitution of the forties and fifties) that is turned inwards, loves national business under protective umbrellas, is hostile to agriculture, and suspicious of free trade. Another version of the same is called *desarrollismo* (developmentalism), which is a misnomer, since it leads, in a global world, to swimming upstream.[26]

The intense and sometimes violent character of Argentine politics has been described as an acute *puja distribucionista* (a distribution fight). The issue, however, is not the form that the conflict takes, but what the conflict is about, for Tweeddledum and Tweeddledee alike. What businessmen, union leaders, public employees, pensioners, the employed, and the unemployed demand is subsidy—a larger portion of protection from the state. The exclusive focus on distribution dampens innovation and entrepreneurship.

The situation is made worse by current demographic trends. Both relative fertility rates and the immigration from poor neighboring countries swell the ranks of people at the bottom of the social pyramid, without a corresponding growth in productive opportunity. Add to this mixture the neglect of infrastructure and of public education, plus the emigration of children from the middle class, and one gets a rough picture of Argentine social decline, with the consequent propensity towards prebendal populism.

In the 1970s a large portion of the middle-class youth took up arms to fight the corrupt distributive system in the name of radical equality, seeking to install in Argentina a regime like Cuba's. They were brutally suppressed by the armed forces, with a policy of *Nacht und Nebel*.[27] State terror produced between 10,000 and 30,000 *desaparecidos*. The military lost power to civilians after the Falklands/Malvinas war. Successor regimes tried, and then amnestied, the generals. Throughout, the survivors and the relatives of the disappeared sought justice for the dead and punishment for the perpetrators. What the survivors dared not say is that, had they 'won,' they were prepared to produce even more victims than the military regime produced. To date, every discussion of the issue that I have witnessed, on the right and on the left, parades only half the truth, and there is no reconciliation. Meanwhile, *justicialista* politics, as usual, has returned to the scene.

The situation has not deteriorated further because of the "tail wind" of commodity exports (with East Asia providing an important stimulus) from agribusiness—precisely the sector that populist politicians have singled out as the target for taxation, which in Argentina takes the form of toll collection at the exit gates. This has produced disinvestment and more social conflict; with the net result that Argentina has ceded competitive ground to Brazil, and even to little Uruguay.

On May 25, 2010 Argentina celebrated a significant birthday—two hundred years of independence. Despite an intense labor of propaganda, the second centennial made a sorry comparison to the first. In 1910 Argentina was one of the most prosperous countries in the world. Today it is a sad sack. For all concerned it is better to look forward than to look back. In this vein, some proposals have begun to circulate, in view not only of the bicentennial, but also of a future change of government in 2012. The more elaborate of these—coming from the thinking opposition—talk of the need for a broad consensus, something like the old Spanish *pacto de la Moncloa*,[28] around long-range policies such as: state stimulus to local industry, the taxation of financial transactions, tax exemptions for profits that are reinvested, a higher and progressive income tax in order to finance universal welfare, and public works in infrastructure. But there is no mention of reducing the high toll imposed on exports (since governments need to skim the cream from rural exports to fund urban welfare), nor changes in immigration policy, since protected industry needs cheap labor from neighboring countries in order to compete with Brazil. The package is protectionist and distributional, with marginal improvements on the existing government plan or *modelo*.

In the 2011 presidential elections, the government—today quite unpopular—may lose, or it may not, since the opposition is a shambles; however, the *Peronista* mindset is likely to remain. The political fight before and after the election could turn nasty,[29] with the firm determination by the losers to make the winners pay a heavy penalty in governance. But the prize remains unchanged: to see who will be in charge of redistribution. Only the hope that the world economy will recover and that Asia will continue to be a prime consumer of Argentine produce, will moderate the *puja distribucionista*, as there will be more to pass around. Is that planning for development? It looks more like limping along. And so the Argentine *justicialista* ship sails on, leaking and listing without sinking, arriving at some ports of refuge and missing many others. Whereas in Cuba the enforcement of radical equality has led to a frozen totalitarian state, in Argentina the Peronist matrix of social justice has produced a bickering variety of corporatism hampering economic growth, which proceeds in fits and starts. Mexico instead is a great country in abeyance. It is caught in the straightjacket of its many monopolies; it concentrates wealth at the top and instead of drawing the poor into a productive fold, it expels them. It may one day become a prosperous partner of the United States if only the internal political dynamics of each partner would allow it. Alas it does not.

Mexico's Impasse

A Day Without Mexicans

In 1994 the City of New York closed all its galleries and museums, effectively instituting "a day without art" to raise public consciousness about the ravages of AIDS in the artistic community. In 1994 Californians were discussing Proposition 187 in view of a referendum. The proposition denied illegal immigrants access to education and health. It was then that Mexican artist Yareli Arizmendi proposed to her husband, the film producer Sergio Arau, to imagine "a day without Mexicans." They made a short film of 28 minutes with that title. Then they shot a longer film, *Un dia sin mexicanos*, which was shown in movie houses in Mexico and the US in 2004.

The film is a satire that portrays what would happen in California if one day its 14 million Hispanics disappeared from the state. In a way the film enacts the dream of the late Professor Samuel Huntington who, in his book *Who Are We? The Challenges to American Identity* also imagined a United States without the alleged cultural threat of Latin American immigration.[30] In the film the state of California is isolated from the Union by a cloud of thick fog. Within the mist, one third of the population is no longer. California is paralyzed. People cry: "There is no food, and no clean dishes!" There are no vegetables and fruits in the markets; gardens are left unattended; children are not taken care of; there is no one to cook or clean latrines, no one to repair roofs, to paint the walls, to pick oranges from trees, to fix the streets. Managers are forced to hire workers at five times the wages of those who vanished. In the end those who remain pray for the return of those who left. The film tries to say: those who are most exploited make good scape goats, but we need them. It is a portrait of bad faith at the receiving end. But what about the sending?

The NAFTA Fiasco

Fifteen years ago the United States reigned supreme as the only superpower. Accordingly, it sought to shape the neighborhood in its own image and after its own needs. And so the North American Free Trade Agreement was born. In the United States, many people assume that Mexico was the big winner from the arrangement. The Mexican government got what it wanted from the agreement: exports to the US increased seven times, much of them in manufacturing. Foreign direct investment rose to four times the level before the deal. It seemed that, with inflation under control and productivity on the rise, the Mexican economy would surge ahead. But it didn't.

Researchers Kevin Gallagher and Timothy Wise explain why:

> The economy grew slowly—an annual rate of 1.6% per capita. This
> was low by historical standards. The economy grew 3.5% per year from
> 1960–79, under the widely criticized policies of "import substitution."
> And it was low by developing country standards. China, India, and
> Brazil all vaulted ahead of Mexico, following a much less orthodox set
> of policies that would be illegal for Mexico under NAFTA. Slow growth
> means limited job creation, all the more so with US exports displacing
> "inefficient" domestic producers. Estimates vary, but Mexico probably
> gained about 600,000 jobs in the manufacturing sector since NAFTA
> took effect, but the country lost at least 2 million in agriculture, as cheap
> imports of corn and other commodities flooded the newly liberalized
> market.[31]

Poor Mexicans continued to move North in search of jobs and a better life,
braving an increasingly militarized and hostile border. Moreover, Mexico's net
loss of employment under NAFTA coincided with the country's baby boom.
One million young people enter the labor force each year—and they don't
find jobs. As a result, the emigration rate doubled during the NAFTA years.

Comparative development shows us that the key to a country's success is
to export goods, not people. On this score, the "associated development" of
Mexico with the United States has been a failure. It was billed however as
a success. The trick consists of defining success only as an increase in trade
and investment. Mexico did get preferential access to the coveted American
market, and capital flowed south of the border. And indeed a concentrated
economy, working for a few, can fare well under this model—only the masses
of people do not. When the crisis struck in the North, the gauge of Mexico's
mediocre growth went negative. Investment stopped, unemployment soared,
and of course, migration lessened, in sync with diminished opportunities in
the US. Remittances slowed to a trickle, and in some cases reversed. What
is wrong with this path of development, that is bad in good times, and in a
crisis worse?

Causes and Solutions

Mexico liberalized its economy and joined the world of American-led
globalization; it failed to break up its huge monopolies, state and private. If
anything, new capital investments and better access to the markets of the
North aggravated economic concentration. The case of Mexico is therefore

one in which inequality is not a byproduct of capitalist development but its impediment. Free markets by themselves only reinforce what exists. In order to liberate their energy, they must be shaped, and this is precisely where the state must intervene—not to redistribute income but to enable socially responsible investments. The "trickle down" effect of concentrated wealth is a will-o'-the-wisp, forever elusive. Only growth from below moves a country forward. Between the hidebound residues of the Mexican revolution, and the neoliberal shakeup that only reshuffled concentrations, the country still awaits a genuine capitalist revolution to enlarge the field of opportunities. Mexican public intellectuals are aware of this, and they have put forth proposals that are well worth examining.

Among them one stands out. In a provocative essay published in the magazine *Nexos*, Jorge Castañeda and Héctor Aguilar Camin write what looks to be a whole program of government, although they deny it.[32] The authors begin by saying that Mexico is imprisoned in the myths of its past—what I refer to as the hidebound residues of the Mexican Revolution. Like Peronism in Argentina, the PRI (Party of the Institutionalized Revolution) has lost its grip on power but keeps its hold of the mind. The sacred cows that Mexicans worship include: energy nationalism, the public ownership of land, the subsoil and the shore, single unions, the rhetorical defense of sovereignty, bureaucratic patrimonialism, and all sorts of corruption disguised with different names. That is quite a path dependency to overcome. Under the influence of these habits and the old vapors of the Mexican revolution, the country stumbles forward, without a clear goal. It pays lip service to an old epic of social justice a thousand times betrayed.

When democracy arrived, the opening was messy and violent, but the rule of a single party ceased, and the opposition won. But like in many other Latin American countries, what was a successful way to power failed as a mode of governance. Mexico made a transition from arbitrary authoritarianism to impotent democracy. For Castañeda and Aguilar Camin, Mexico suffers from an excess of past and a deficit of future. These and other public intellectuals would like to use the presidential elections of 2012 as a referendum on a new course of development. Their guiding idea is a prosperous society with a large ascending middle class. They propose a set of reforms to make this possible: economic, geopolitical, institutional, and some in the domain of rights.

The logic of reform is the liberation of productive forces from the shackles of monopolies and corporatism. Once growth is energized, other reforms must insure its fair distribution—social justice can be attained but without killing in the process the goose that lays the eggs. People should be given tools, not fruits, not fish but fishing rods. And a paramount tool is education. Without repeating the details of the authors' proposal, I should note that its essence is the productive mobilization of the middle strata and the progressive access of the poor to that status.

None of this is possible without unleashing economic growth, so as to pass the threshold of 6 per cent with which the tide can lift all boats. And such growth is not possible in turn without the breakup of Mexican monopolies, which are a form of frozen redistribution—corporatism as a form of social justice. It would probably require a visionary subgroup of the elite to carry out an anti-trust program of such magnitude—a Mexican Teddy Roosevelt helped by technocrats.

The proposers of this strategy do not mince words: Mexico, as the saying goes, is too far from God and too close to the United States. That cannot be changed, but it can be turned into an opportunity, which it has not been thus far. 90 per cent of Mexican trade is with the United States, 70 per cent of foreign investment comes from the US, 1 million Americans live in Mexico and 12 million Mexicans in the United States. Half of all Mexicans have a relative or two living in the North; one third would like to live there. Yet neither in Mexico nor in the United States the political elites are intelligent enough to try a comprehensive plan of integration. On both sides of the borders chauvinists sound strident. They prefer, as many special interests do, to profit from stagnation and sheer cant.

Mexico must break up its archaic institutions—not just breaking up trusts but corporatist unions as well. The United States must restore what experts call "circularity" in its approach to immigration. But the key remains in Mexico: How to unleash the economic pent-up energy of its middle class? If it fails in this historic undertaking, it will follow in the footsteps of Argentina, and fall behind Brazil. Will anyone who politically counts in Mexico have the guts to declare, in 2012, that the goal is to launch a true "bourgeois revolution" at home and seek comprehensive integration with the economies of the North?

This chapter sought to show that south of the crisis things look problematic but not too dire. Progress in the years ahead in these four cases would mean—in the best possible scenario: for Cuba, to shake its torpor and follow a "Vietnamese way"; for Brazil, to energize from government the entrepreneurial aspirations of its new middle class; for Argentina, to overcome the Peronist syndrome and take a page from Chile and another from Brazil; and for Mexico, to break up the monopolies and integrate intelligently with the North. The different ways out have one theme in common: socially inclusive capitalist growth.

Chapter Ten

THE CHALLENGE OF INCLUSION

The Policies that Nobody Wants?

So far Latin America has been spared the worst of the crisis. Economists concur in thinking that for the region the crisis has been more a problem in trade than a financial stranglehold. However, the evolution of the global economy indicates that Latin American countries too should take rational prudential measures in the second decade of the century. This runs counter, of course, to the political needs of the moment that lead governments to spend more than they should in periods of elections. Moreover, at the global level itself—in the central economies—the rescue measures that were originally taken have been partial and shy. By leaving culprit institutions in place, they end up fostering a return to the dubious practice of speculation; they promote the further concentration of wealth and power; and they leave in the shadow of a weak recovery hundreds of millions of people who wish to work but can't. The appropriate slogan for this "recovery" should be "more of the same" or "let's fall forward."

In this rather somber context of recovery with slow growth, big unemployment, and greater social inequality in two thirds of the world, we may anticipate an even worse crisis in the future. It is no longer just Japan that faces a "lost decade," but the United States and Europe as well. These economic zones have not yet left the danger of deflation behind them, or the risk of a dispiriting combination of deflation and inflation (stagflation) for a considerable period of time.

In Latin America the prospects are rosier, based on two factors—one is structural and the other circumstantial. Favorable circumstances rest on the expectation that the new motor of economic growth will be in East Asia, and in China in particular. In geopolitical terms, what drives the absolute necessity of fast growth in China? The answer is simple, even brutal: China is on a race to become rich before it becomes old. The other Asian nations follow behind. But to bet on this prospect on the part of Latin Americans is to put too many eggs in one basket without knowing the basket too well. It is an article of faith. In any event, it is highly probable that Asian markets will increase their demand for industrial inputs and foodstuffs, and such circumstances augur well for the economies of the South. But the projected favorable circumstances assume the same structure of the world economy.

If, however, a prolonged stagnation in the central economies puts an end to the Chinese model of vendor finance, the Chinese leadership will have to turn inwards and launch policies of societal inclusion and internal prosperity to keep the economy humming. This could take place in two ways: first by the rise in purchasing power of the coastal population, and second by moving the current frontier of breakneck growth with cheap labor further west, to the more remote hinterland, thus completing the transformation of farmers and peasants into an industrial workforce. None of this is easy, and the ensuing dislocation may produce serious unrest. That is how, in an interdependent world, disorder in a remote province of China may affect the cash flow of Latin American governments.

Given these considerations, the post-crisis world has several options before it. One option I have already named "more of the same." It is convenient; it does not upset the apple cart of those who benefit from the present system, and puts everybody else at ease, because "better the Devil you know than the Devil you don't." A crisis is always a trauma. For many the fear of the unknown dims the imagination and dumbs down thought. This first scenario leaves structures intact, and hence the near certainty of new crises down the road.

Structural reforms instead are reforms for the long haul. Without them, we can say once more that those who forget history are condemned to repeat it. The warnings of this type come from prestigious figures of the international financial regulatory establishment. I shall mention a few. Tomasso Padoa-Schioppa, president of *Our Europe* (a research center founded by Jacques Delors) and a former Minister of the Economy in Italy, is a central banker in Rome and Frankfurt and an officer of the European Commission. In a book titled *La veduta corta* (*The Short Sight*),[1] he castigates the limited purview of the markets (always after quick profits), of governments (always minding the next election), of the media (keen on sensationalist news and on their ratings), of business enterprises, of families, and of popular psychology in general. Without a calmer, long-range perspective, without the distant view of the whole (not the speedy view of the airplane moving on the runway but the soaring view of high altitudes), Padoa-Schioppa contends that our society is condemned to live constantly at risk, jumping from one crisis to the next. Also in Europe, Jacques Attali, former head of the European Development Bank and former adviser to François Mitterrand, holds similar opinions.[2]

In the United States a number of very distinguished economists (two of them Nobel Prize winners) are also critical of current policies, which they deem complacent and supportive of the status quo. They have moved away from the assumptions of their discipline. But the strongest view comes from the former chairman of the Federal Reserve in previous times of turbulence, Paul Volcker. In an Op Ed article published in *The New York Times*,[3] Volcker argues, that the large banking conglomerates like Citibank should break up their different operations, putting "firewalls" between them; and that in case of a new financial crisis, the government should preside over the liquidation of the large banking houses. In other words, for Paul Volcker, the financial institutions that are deemed "too large to fail" are too, in fact, large to exist. In a modernized version, Volcker repeats the recommendation of Adam Smith in *The Wealth of Nations*, that banks should be small.

More recently, Martin Wolf has reasoned on the various scenarios of "exit" and has come to the conclusion that the prevailing strategies will only prolong a sluggish and unequal development for years to come, and he seeks answers in the more radical critiques of the model of growth that led to the crisis in the first place.[1] The problem is that radical solutions are the solutions that established groups fear most. In the end, only a surge in private and public investments in the deficit countries and a surge in demand in the emerging ones can pull the global economy from the doldrums. That puts a heavy burden on the public sector in the former and a shift in priorities in the latter. The paradox is this. There is a glut of funds in the public sector but no willingness to invest in a society mired now in the reduction of debt. How to channel these funds in investments, both public and private across the world? This agenda involves no less than a conscious reduction of inequality on a planetary scale.

A strategy that goes beyond propping up the status quo would be more rational and would have a better chance of success. But this second option is comprehensive and ambitious: It means the technocratic and international regulation of the financial sector (coordinated among the industrialized and the emergent nations, nowadays grouped in the G-20), coupled with an aggressive policy of social protection for the populations that loses jobs and homes. It would entail a new New Deal.

The obstacles to such strategy are strong and many. They stem from a basic fact: the world has not made yet a full transition from geopolitics to geo-economics. National interests trump the common interest. The latter staggers in zigzags, between unfulfilled promises and treatises that do not mean much.

There is no doubt in my mind that the rational planning strategy is more attractive and sane than anything we have seen so far, because it anticipates problems and manages risk. It is the position of President Obama, but only in a philosophical sense. In practice he finds it very difficult to convince politicians in both parties and the citizenry at large that rational state intervention is not all bad. From economic controls to social security and health, his policies are either diluted or blocked. Europe, in turn, has the opposite problem: it has a single currency without a single government. In the various European countries, however, the legacy of social democracy means that the very same institutions that in periods of economic bonanza act as a brake on fast growth, in periods of crisis act as parachutes to slow the fall.

A third possible scenario in this repertoire of exits from the crisis is perhaps the worst of all: it is one of more crises and fragmentation. Under conditions of prolonged stagnation and financial duress, countries could be tempted to withdraw into their own defensive cocoons. Regional, national, and local autarky can only lead to international anarchy and to tensions that could ultimately produce wars. Confrontation and conflict would define such world.[5]

Each of the scenarios presented above is only an ideal type; an abstract stylization of what in reality is a more complex and messy world. What we are likely to get is a combination of them, most likely in sequence, as in a musical piece. But we cannot bet on a good orchestral arrangement.

Towards Social Inclusion

The underlying thesis of this book is that the deep source of trouble is the excessive concentration of wealth and the exclusion of majorities from the mobilization of their productive potential. Latin America—hitherto the most unequal region of the world—could, precisely because of that, lead the way by showing, through intelligent initiatives, that the reduction of inequality can lead to prosperity and to the elimination of dire poverty. As in other matters of policy, there are good and bad ways of seeking this goal. A short-term view (la veduta corta) leads politicians to sacrifice growth in order to get votes. Such tactics lead to temporary welfare but long-run decline. Populism and clientelism are convenient tools to acquire power or to stay in it. What the countries need, instead, are investments in education, infrastructure, tax simplification, and the breakup of monopolies of all sorts.

Unfortunately, both in the North and in the South, the larger rational view has few followers. The gap is wide between intention and practice, between the many politicians and the scant men and women of state.

What is inclusive development? Inclusion is a process and a goal that seeks to reduce inequalities: not all inequalities, but those that are extreme, and those that prevent groups of people from progressing in the generation of wealth. Why is the reduction of inequalities important? Because when inequality and wealth concentration run amuck, they generate systemic crises—which, in turn, often result in even greater wealth concentration. And so a gigantic vicious circle is produced. I have argued in this book that top-down, forced equalization creates more problems than it solves—in particular it leads to stagnation and demoralization. That is the price of radical revolution. Populism is another defective attempt at reducing inequalities. Mere redistribution is revolution on the cheap—profligate todays and sorrowful tomorrows. How then to mitigate inequality without sacrificing initiative and wealth creation? How to equitably distribute life chances in a sustainable way?

As mentioned before in this book, complex social systems generate categorical distinctions. The problem arises when people are excluded from the process and the fruits of development because of these differences, and when a scalar difference is so extreme that it becomes categorical. The latter can be due to a range of factors, some universal, some culturally specific. Inclusion is about society changing to accommodate difference, and to combat discrimination. To achieve inclusion, a double approach is needed: focusing on the society to remove the barriers that exclude, and focusing on the groups of persons who are excluded, to build their capacity and support them in joining the mainstream. Inclusive development, therefore, is a process that insures that all excluded or marginalized groups are included in the creation of wealth.

The United Nations Millennium Development Goals provide a basic framework:

- Eradicate extreme poverty and hunger
- Achieve universal primary education
- Promote gender equality and empower women
- Reduce child mortality
- Improve maternal health
- Ensure environmental sustainability
- Develop a global partnership for development

Key ingredients in these goals are the alleviation of poverty, the promotion of human rights, and the participation of civil society. But the Millennium Goals provide only a general framework. The important task is to translate these goals into more specific proposals, plans, and initiatives. Here I should like to mention some bottom-up tools that are being tried in various countries of Latin America, not to "abolish" inequality but to raise the level of opportunity, so that all, and not just a few, can play the developmental game.

Latin America today is a relatively calm region in a world in serious turmoil. As opposed to previous crises, this one is much bigger but not endogenous. For Latin American countries the crisis is a context. But their reprieve is temporary. It would be tragic if it led, on the part of leaders at all levels—governmental, entrepreneurial, political, and civic—to complacency or worse, to a posture of defiant adventurism. The world crisis offers Latin American countries an opportunity to prepare for a change in course. It is important to use the context of crisis to accelerate transformative actions designed to abate wealth concentration, inequity, poverty, and above all, to equip people with tools, tangible and intangible, to improve their lot. What are the types of action to find a sustainable way out?

In a recent book on the paths of exit from the crisis, Argentine economist Roberto Mizrahi proposes three general strategies.[6] First, at the macroeconomic level (the level of state policies), he proposes a package of fiscal, public-spending, monetary, credit, investment, and R&D policies that could transform the concentration-oriented growth pattern of Latin American economies. In fiscal policy the abolition of regressive taxation is indispensable, as is the abolition of easy-to-collect revenues that create conflict and reduce incentives. In terms of public spending, he proposes a shift in priorities, concentrating expenditures on services for the underserved, while leaving private investment to satisfy the needs of upper income groups. Monetary policy in turn, should be aimed at price stability, so that credit can flow to lower income sectors of the population. Monetary and fiscal policy should have the goal of channeling capital, knowledge, contacts, and information to the bottom of the productive system.

At the mesoeconomic level (the level of companies' strategies), this author proposes a plan for large corporations to take into account the impact of their business decisions on the other players within the production network they lead. "This implies ensuring sustainability to suppliers, distributors, and those who buy their products, be these supplies, capital goods, or consumer goods. This is about fostering, in the companies, a systemic vision of their own development, so as to minimize negative externalities and use the positive ones for the benefit of their whole productive network and the communities they operate in."[7]

Last but not least, Mizrahi proposes an integrated business-promotion approach at the local level (the level of communities), where small producers are eager to participate but are scattered and disconnected from longer chains of value. This is the most innovative part of the proposal. The tools range from micro lending to business developers, to local venture capital funds, to networks of angel investors. The narrative on the life and fate of these initiatives makes fascinating reading. Here I will emphasize only the overall objective: to provide the excluded poor the economic tools with which to join the ranks of the middle class.

Late capitalism, now in deep crisis, has long left its moorings in the real life of communities, has concentrated wealth in extreme fashion, has perverted its old values, and has eroded the life-world. It is high time to rein it back to serve the nobler purpose of social entrepreneurialism and development with solidarity.

NOTES

Preface

1. The concept of late capitalism has been in circulation at least since the publication of Natalia Moszkowa, *Zur Dynamik des Spätkapitalismus* (Zurich: Verlag Der Aufbruch, 1943). The name has been in use among Marxists, critical theorists, and cultural commentators. In a very general sense it denotes a stage in the development of the world economy dominated by the fluidities of financial capital. A most recent critical formulation of the structural problems of late capitalism is in *The Corruption of Capitalism: A Strategy to Rebalance the Global Economy and Restore Sustainable Growth*, Richard Duncan (Hong Kong: CLSA, 2009). See also *Bad Money: Reckless Finance, Failed Politics, and the Global Crisis of American Capitalism*, Kevin Phillips (New York: Viking, 2008).
2. As presented by Colin Crouch, *Post-Democracy* (Cambridge: Polity Press, 2004).

Introduction

1. As argued by Martin van Creveld, *The Changing Face of War: Lessons of Combat, from the Marne to Iraq* (New York: Presidio Press, 2007).
2. From the perspective of what Ferdinand Braudel called *la longue durée*, which gives priority to long-term historical structures over events, China is not, as some believe, a "newcomer" but a "returner."
3. When Ronald Reagan and Mikhail Gorbachev met in Reykjavik, Iceland, in 1986, Soviet officials warned their American counterparts, "We have deprived you of an enemy."
4. In the 1980s Latin American nations got into very serious debt crises. As Latin America's economies stagnated (experiencing zero or negative economic growth), per capita income plummeted, poverty increased, and the already wide gap between the rich and the poor widened further. The debt crises seriously eroded whatever gains had been made in reducing poverty through improved social welfare measures over the preceding three decades. These developments led policymakers to label the 1980s "the lost decade of development." With few exceptions (notably Chile), the structural adjustments that followed in the 1990s failed to generate sustainable growth and in many instances ended up in even worse debacles—like the Argentine default of 2001. See Carol Wise and Riordan Roett, eds., *Post-Stabilization Politics in Latin America: Competition, Transition, Collapse* (Washington, DC: Brookings Institution, 2003).
5. Jorge Luis Borges, "El jardín de los senderos que se bifurcan," *Ficciones* (Buenos Aires: Emecé, 1941).
6. Max Weber, *The Methodology of the Social Sciences* (Glencoe, IL: The Free Press, 1949).

7. Andrés Malamud, "Liderança sem seguidores: O controverso status do Brasil como potência" ["Leadership Without Followers: The Contested Case for Brazilian Power Status"] (paper presented at the XXVIII International Congress of the Latin American Studies Association, Rio de Janeiro, June 11–14, 2009).

8. Carol Wise, "No Turning Back: Trade Integration and the New Development Mandate," in *Requiem or Revival: The Promise of North American Integration,* eds. Isabel Studer and Carol Wise, 1–23 (Washington, DC: Brookings Institution, 2007).

9. "This Latin quote is from verse 69 of the first book and the first of the satires of Horace. [It] revolves around the subject of avarice. Having painted a grim picture of the greedy person, comparing him to Tantalus, Horace then exclaimed '*Quid rides? Mutato nomine, de te fabula narratur*'—which translates… 'Why are you laughing? Change the name, and the story [is about you].'" Online: http://everything2.com/title/ (accessed 5 May 2010).

10. Kevin Phillips, *Bad Money: Reckless Finance, Failed Politics, and the Global Crisis of American Capitalism* (New York: Viking, 2008). Phillips argues that financial recklessness, combined with peak oil and the rise of Asian economic power, will doom American world leadership and standard of living.

11. José Antonio Ocampo, *La crisis financiera mundial y su impacto sobre América Latina* (New York: United Nations Development Program, 2009); and Pablo Gerchunoff, "Las crisis económicas mundiales y su impacto en Amércia Latina," in *Nueva agenda económico social para América Latina* (Buenos Aires: 2008), 50–60.

12. Path dependency is the view that change in a society depends quantitatively and/or qualitatively on its own past.

13. On the roots and consequences of inequality, see Charles Tilly, *Durable Inequality* (Berkeley: University of California Press, 1998).

14. See "Special Issue on Global Inequality," *Journal of World-Systems Research* 8, no. 1 (Winter 2002).

15. Jennifer Wheary, Thomas M. Shapiro, and Tamara Draut, *By a Thread: The New Experience of America's Middle Class* (Waltham, MA: Demos/IASP, 2007).

16. For the case of Argentina, see Alberto Minujin, *La clase media seducida y abandonada* (Buenos Aires: Edhasa, 2004).

17. Juan E. Corradi, "The Food Chain," *Opinión Sur* 61 (September 2008).

18. Kevin Phillips, "Numbers Racket: Why the Economy Is Worse Than We Know," *Harper's Magazine,* May 2008, 43–47. In either crude or sophisticated ways, governments tend to dissimulate negative statistics, especially those pertaining to inflation.

19. Paul Krugman, "The Third Depression," *The New York Times,* Op-Ed, June 27, 2010.

20. Gerchunoff, *loc. cit.*

21. For a portrait of the period from a biographical point of view, see Edgar J. Dosman, *The Life and Times of Raúl Prebisch, 1901–1986* (Montreal: McGill-Queen's University Press, 2008).

22. Robert Cyran and Antony Currie, "China's Growth, Measured in Feed," *The New York Times,* sec. B2, January 28, 2010.

23. Short-term populist measures designed to yield electoral dividends do hamper longer-term and sustainable growth. Argentina and Venezuela are cases in point.

24. As presented in Chapter Five, this is one of the main challenges in the "Chimericas" model.

25. Dani Rodrik, *One Economics, Many Recipes: Globalization, Institutions, and Economic Growth* (Princeton: Princeton University Press, 2008).

26. The periodic meetings of the G-20 only produce weak manifestos of agreed-upon general principles. They confirm Napoleon's cynical remark: "Principles are fine. They do not commit us to anything."

Chapter One: Impending Storms

1. Consumer spending, valued at $11 trillion, represents two-thirds of the North American economy. This is also, coincidentally, the amount owed to foreign creditors. Economists have long maintained that the United States acts as the global economy's "locomotive." This situation will persist until the day when China, with a billion potential consumers, becomes the world's principal economy.

2. It is very probable that in the future the dollar will cease to be the only reserve currency. The world economy will move to a tripartite system of reserve currencies: the dollar, the euro, and the yuan. This system will be part of a new "multipolar" world order already heralded by the French president.

3. The Argentines' reasoning was not far off the mark. In the United States, the average family spends 13 per cent of its earnings, after taxes, to service its debts. The bulk of this money goes towards paying back mortgages and car loans, but aside from that, each family has on average $8,000 in credit card debt, which carries a much higher interest rate. What is at stake is nothing less than the future of the North American middle class, the mainstay of national identity. Today more than 75 per cent of middle-class family income is dedicated to covering fixed expenses (mortgage, car loans, child care, health insurance, and taxes) compared with only 50 per cent of income thirty years ago.

4. My own estimate was that, for the time being, the Federal Reserve would let the dollar continue to lose value, in spite of the reticence of the Central European Bank and the Bank of Japan. When it reached a floor of $1.40 per euro, the political pressure for coordinated intervention from the North's central banks would become stronger. But, we could not rule out an even greater drop. However, this estimate was made on the condition that other things would be equal, which they seldom are. If some members of the Euro zone defaulted like Argentina once did, or bolted out of the union, all those bets would be off.

5. A Chinese strategist introduced the concept of a "fictitious economy." See Wang Jian, "The American War: A Chinese View," in *The Value of Singapore* (2003).

6. Joseph E. Stiglitz and Linda J. Bilmes, *The Three Trillion Dollar War: The True Cost of the Iraq Conflict* (New York: Norton, 2008).

7. The social ground for third-party movements is for the moment heterogeneous. It defines itself in terms of reflexive reaction against the elite's (of both principal parties) defining ideas and proclivities, such as higher taxes and expanding government, social engineering, approval of abortion, alternative families, and secularism. Many want to restore a way of life largely superseded. The American Tea Party movement is a case in point.

8. Edward Luce, "Goodbye, American Dream," *Financial Times*, August 1, 2010.

9. For a confirmation of the views in this chapter, see Paul Kennedy, "The Dollar's Fate," *The New York Times*, Op-Ed, August 29, 2009; and especially "The World Supremacy of the Dollar at the Rendering (1917–2008)," Antonio Mosconi, *The New Federalist.eu*, October 2, 2009. Online: http://www.thenewfederalist.eu/The-World-Supremacy-of-the-Dollar-at-the-Rendering-1917–2008 (accessed January 5, 2010).

10. A repeat scenario of Argentina in 2001 is Greece in 2010, see James Rickards, "How Markets Attacked the Greek Piñata," *Financial Times*, February 12, 2010.

Chapter Two: The Troubles at the Center

1. In *One Economics, Many Recipes: Globalization, Institutions, and Economic Growth*, the leading developmental economist Dani Rodrik argues that while economic globalization can be a boon for countries that are trying to dig out of poverty, success usually requires following policies that are tailored to local economic and political realities rather than obeying the dictates of the international globalization establishment.

2. Joseph Stiglitz, "How to Get Out of the Financial Crisis," *Time*, October 17, 2008. Online: http://www.time.com/time/business/article/0,8599,1851739,00.html.

3. Robert B. Zoellick, "A World in Crisis Means a Chance for Greatness," *The Washington Post*, October 26, 2008.

4. Phillips, *Bad Money*, op.cit.

5. F. Serrano, "A economia Americana, o padrão 'dólar-flexivel' e a expansão mundial nos anos 2000," in *O Mito do Colapso Americano*, eds. J.L., Fiori, F. Serrano, and C. Medeiros (Rio de Janeiro: Editora Record, 2008).

6. To understand how this system works, see Maurice Obstfeld, and Kenneth Rogoff, "Global Current Account Imbalances and Exchange Rate Adjustments," *Brookings Papers on Economic Activity* 1 (2005): 67–146.

7. Wolfgang Schivelbusch, *Three New Deals: Reflections on Roosevelt's America, Mussolini's Italy, and Hitler's Germany, 1933–1939* (New York: Metropolitan Books, 2006); and Doris Kearns Goodwin, *No Ordinary Time: Franklin and Eleanor Roosevelt; The Home Front in World War II* (New York: Simon & Schuster, 1994).

8. The revival of the political thought of Carl Schmitt, and following in his footsteps, the work of Italian theorist Giorgio Agamben register, in the halls of academia, the "spirit of the times." *Homo Sacer: Sovereign Power and Bare Life by Giorgio Agamben*, trans. Daniel Heller-Roazen (Stanford, CA: Stanford University Press, 1998).

9. It is interesting to note how those in the "rebel," petro-state capitals—whether Moscow, Tehran, or Caracas—who rail most vehemently against Western capitalism reduce their rhetoric every time the price of oil, or commodities in general, drops. At the same time, it must be noted that the Southern countries continue to finance the deficit in the Northern countries by investing their accumulated export reserves rather than applying them to their own markets. The surplus funds are deposited in the US and the European Union.

10. A very good study on the characteristics and evolution of Chinese capitalism, particularly the continued role of the state, is Yasheng Huang, *Capitalism with Chinese Characteristics: Entrepreneurship and the State* (Cambridge and New York: Cambridge University Press, 2008).

11. Translation: I speak and write a bit of Swedish.

12. Notably Martin van Creveld, *The Changing Face of War: Lessons of Combat, from the Marne to Iraq* (New York: Presidio Press, 2007).

13. Ulrich Beck, *Risk Society: Towards a New Modernity* (London: Sage Publications, 1992). Originally published as *Risikogesellschaft: Auf dem Weg in eine andere Moderne*, (Frankfurt am Main: Suhrkamp Verlag, 1986).

14. The strip of coastal land that encircles Eurasia. Classic geostrategists like Sir Halford J. Mackinder and Nicholas J. Spykman debated its importance.

15. This is war as defined in *On War* by Carl von Clausewitz, trans. and ed. Michael Howard and Peter Paret (Princeton: Princeton University Press, 1984); and redefined by Martin van Creveld, *The Transformation of War: The Most Radical Reinterpretation of Armed Conflict since Clausewitz* (New York: The Free Press, 1991).

Chapter Three: The Response

1. For a succinct description of the policies leading to catastrophic crisis in Argentina, see Tulio Halperin Donghi, "Why Did Argentina Adopt a Neoliberal Model?" in *Argentina in Collapse? The Americas Debate*, eds., Michael Cohen and Margarita Gutman (New York: The New School, 2002).

2. Being saved or drowning will ultimately depend upon the strength and direction of the current. Strong or weak, favorable or unfavorable, currents are global. The success or failure of the policies depends, to a great extent, on the way they are adapted to these currents. I believe it appropriate to point out that, unlike other regions, the impact of the world on Latin America has always been greater than that of Latin America on the world—despite the continent's geographic and demographic volume. Suffice it to remember Churchill's witty remark about the impact of the small Balkan states on international balance, and then reverse it: "They produce more history than they are capable of consuming." By contrast, Latin America consumes more history than it is capable of producing. Hegel first made that reflection about Latin America.

3. Juan Carlos Torre, *El proceso político de las reformas económicas en América Latina* (Buenos Aires-Barcelona-México: Paidos, 1998), 40 (my translation).

4. For the impact of the "generation YouTube" on American politics, see Morley Winograd and Michael D. Hais, *Millennial Makeover: MySpace, YouTube, and the Future of American Politics* (New Brunswick, NJ and London: Rutgers University Press, 2008).

5. James MacGregor Burns, *Roosevelt: The Lion and the Fox* (New York: Harcourt Brace, 1956), 166–167.

6. Mordechai Benyakar, *Lo disruptivo: Amenazas individuales y colectivas: el psiquismo ante guerras, terrorismos y catástrofes sociales* (Buenos Aires: Biblos, 2003).

7. A classic essay on the politics of fear is by Franz Neumann, "Anxiety and Politics," in *The Democratic and the Authoritarian State* (edited with an introduction by Herbert Marcuse, Glencoe, IL: The Free Press 1957).

8. Especially the novels of the 1960s Latin American "boom" writers: Alejo Carpentier, Gabriel García Márquez, Arturo Roa Bastos, Edmundo Desnoes, Carlos Fuentes, and Mario Vargas Llosa.

9. See the classic argument by Max Horkheimer, *Eclipse of Reason* (New York: Oxford University Press, Continuum International Publishing Group, 1947).

10. Paul Krugman, "The Third Depression," *The New York Times*, Op-Ed, June 27, 2010.

11. Kondratiev waves are described as regular, sinusoidal-like cycles in the modern (capitalist) world economy. Averaging fifty and ranging from approximately forty to sixty years in length, the cycles consist of alternating periods between high sectoral growth and periods of relatively slow growth.

12. Despite a statistical "recovery" of economic activity, the evolution of unemployment in the US is alarming, as revealed in a dynamic chart, "The Decline: The Geography of a Recession," produced by labor writer and journalist Latoya Egwuekwe. Online: http:// latoyaegwuekwe.wordpress.com/ (accessed February 5, 2010). A recovery without social inclusion (or rather with social exclusion) is unsustainable.

13. I do not mention the Argentine meltdown of 2001–2 because Argentina is such an exceptional case, and has been for most of the last century. For a good description of the crisis and its aftermath, see Eduardo Levy Yeyati and Diego Valenzuela, *La resurrección: Historia de la poscrisis argentina* (Buenos Aires: Editorial Sudamericana, 2007).

14. On modalities of "cooking the books," see the video-taped conference by Kevin Phillips. Online: http://video.google.com/videoplay?docid=3035415655640961960#/.

15. Even given this standard indicator (GDP), economists have a lot to answer for. There is a widening gap between data (as hitherto measured) and reality that distorts the official picture of a country's economic health, overstating growth and productivity. The statistical distortions are significant. In fact, the American GDP would have risen at only 3.3 per cent annual rate in the third quarter instead of the 3.5 per cent reported if more accurate measures had been chosen. At a recent conference on economic indicators, experts pointed to the failure to distinguish between what is made in the US and what is made abroad, thus falsely inflating the gross domestic product. Moreover, because overstated value added is accompanied by great job losses in the current downturn, the overvalued products appear as produced by fewer workers, and productivity falsely rises. In this way official statistics turn a bad situation into an apparent good one.

16. See the interesting study by Wolfgang Schivelbusch, *Three New Deals: Reflections on Roosevelt's America, Mussolini's Italy, and Hitler's Germany, 1933–1939* (New York: Metropolitan Books, 2006).

17. Credit default swaps (CDS) are a financial instrument for swapping the risk of debt default. CDS may be used for emerging market bonds, mortgage backed securities, corporate bonds, and local government bond. The buyer of a credit default swap pays a premium for effectively insuring against a debt default. She or he receives a lump sum payment if the debt instrument is defaulted. The seller of a credit default swap receives monthly payments from the buyer. If the debt instrument defaults they have to pay the agreed amount to the buyer of the credit default swap. CDS are dangerous instruments in unscrupulous hands, as the following analogy makes clear: it is as if your neighbors were allowed to purchase fire insurance on the potential burning of your home.

18. Among the best studies are Carmen M. Reinhart and Kenneth S. Rogoff, "Part VI: What Have We Learned?" in *This Time is Different: Eight Centuries of Financial Folly* (Princeton: Princeton University Press, 2009); and Nouriel Roubini and Stephen Mihm, *Crisis Economics: A Crash Course in the Future of Finance* (New York: Penguin Press, 2010).

19. Rudolf Hilferding, *Finance Capital: A Study of the Latest Phase of Capitalist Development* (London: Routledge & Kegan Paul, 1985); and Vladimir I. Lenin, *Selected Works* (Moscow: Progress Publishers, 1963), 1: 667–766.

20. A strategy in which an investor sells a certain currency with a relatively low interest rate and uses the funds to purchase a different currency yielding a higher interest rate.

21. Jan Petter Myklebust, "Scandinavia: Reforms Continue Despite Crisis," *University World News*, March 21, 2010.

22. Roberto S. Mizrahi, *International Crisis: Adjusting the Course and Improving the Systemic Functioning* (Buenos Aires: Editorial Opinión Sur, 2009).

23. For the predicament in Europe, see Jacques Attali, *Tous ruinés dans dix ans? Dette publique: la dernière chance* (Paris: Fayard, 2010).

24. On Chinese intellectuals, see Cui Zhiyuan, *Second Liberation of Thought* (Hong Kong: Oxford University Press, 1997); for more general discussion, see Mark Leonard, *What Does China Think?* (London: Fourth Estate, 2008); for Chinese views of long-term

strategy, see Yang Yi, "Occupying the Moral Height of Enriching Our Country and Empowering our Military," translated by Zhang Feng, *Global Times*, April 27, 2006; and see the much-cited book by Qiao Liang and Wang Xiangsu, *Unrestricted Warfare* (Beijing: PLA Literature and Arts Publishing House, 1999).

25. Anna Maria Jaguaribe, "Visões de Futuro: A China e seus desafios, elementos do debate atual," unpublished paper (Rio de Janeiro, 2009).

26. The Danes are taking the lead in these experiments. See the link to Cluster Biofuels Denmark, probably the most visionary sustainable energy organization in the land. Online: http://www.cbd-denmark.dk/index.php?language=en/.

Chapter Four: A Paucity of Thought and Action

1. There are honorable exceptions, among them New York University's Stern School's Nouriel Roubini. See the profile by Jonathan Sibun, "Nouriel Roubini said the bubble would burst and it did. So what next? The dismal science? Don't believe a word of it," *Telegraph*, May 23, 2010.

2. Oft-cited works include John Maynard Keynes, *The Great Slump of 1930* (London: The Nation & Athenæum, 1930); Irving Fisher, "The Debt-Deflation Theory of Great Depressions," *Econometrica* 1 (October 1933): 337–357; and Hyman P. Minsky, *Can "It" Happen Again? Essays on Instability and Finance* (Armonk, NY: M. E. Sharpe, 1982).

3. There are few but very distinguished critics—some of them received the accolade of the Nobel Prize. They came from the mainstream of the economics profession but later veered from it and do not mince words. Joseph Stiglitz, Paul Krugman, and Amartya Sen are the best-known names. The most comprehensive understanding of the crisis is from historians who have turned their attention to finance, like Niall Ferguson, *The Ascent of Money: A Financial History of the World* (New York: Penguin Press, 2008); or economists who have turned their attention to history, like Carmen M. Reinhart and Kenneth S. Rogoff, *This Time is Different: Eight Centuries of Financial Folly* (Princeton: Princeton University Press, 2009). A precedent for their work can be found in the work of a brilliant gadfly much maligned by the hard-liners in the profession, namely, John Kenneth Galbraith, *A Short History of Financial Euphoria* (New York: Penguin, 1994); and in the classic text by Charles P. Kindleberger and Robert Aliber, *Manias, Panics, and Crashes: A History of Financial Crises*, 5th edition (Hoboken, NJ: Wiley, 2005). See also Robert F. Bruner and Sean D. Carr, *The Panic of 1907: Lessons Learned from the Market's Perfect Storm* (Hoboken, NJ: Wiley, 2007).

4. See Gosta Esping-Andersen, *Social Foundations of Postindustrial Economies* (New York and London: Oxford University Press, 1999). This author distinguishes between several different *homines*: *homo liberalis*, *homo families*, and *homo socialdemocraticus*.

5. For more on this issue, see John Mankoff and Verónica Montecinos, "El irresistible ascenso de los economistas," *Desarrollo Económico: Revista de Ciencias Sociales* 133 (April–June 1994).

6. In this respect, the discipline of economics deserves the internal bashing that sociology received from C. Wright Mills, *The Sociological Imagination* (Oxford: Oxford University Press, 1959).

7. The sociologist Robert K. Merton made this point in 1949 in a seminal collection of essays titled *Social Theory and Social Structure* (Glencoe, IL: The Free Press, 1949). He was the father of Robert C. Merton, who received (with Myron Scholes) the Nobel Prize

in economics in 1997, before the current crisis, *"for a new method to determine the value of derivatives."* The method was highly lucrative.

8. See Craig Calhoun, "Is the University in Crisis?" *Society* (May–June 2006): 8–18.

9. See Jacques Attali, *La crise, et après?* (Paris: Fayard, 2008).

10. Kevin Phillips, *Bad Money: Reckless Finance, Failed Politics, and the Global Crisis of American Capitalism* (New York: Viking, 2008).

11. It is not difficult to foresee such a catastrophe. For a dismal scenario, see Jacques Attali, *Tous ruinés dans dix ans? Dette publique: la dernière chance* (Paris: Fayard, 2010).

12. Simon Johnson, "The Quiet Coup," *The Atlantic*, March 27, 2009.

13. "Masters of the Universe" refers to the directors of the big investment banks, hedge funds (part of the extra-bank financial sector), and insurance companies on Wall Street, whose insolence must be endured in city restaurants, at benefit parties, in their Greenwich mansions in winter and their Hamptons oceanfront estates in the summer. Business schools have been transformed, from training grounds for socially responsible executives to incubators for young speculators whose talents are fed with greed. For an excellent analysis of this transformation, see Rakesh Khurana, *From Higher Aims to Hired Hands: The Social Transformation of American Business Schools and the Unfulfilled Promise of Management as a Profession* (Princeton: Princeton University Press, 2007).

14. Julián Martel [José María Miró], *La Bolsa: Estudio social*, Segunda edición (Buenos Aires: Imprenta artística "Buenos Aires," 1891).

15. Louis D. Brandeis, *Other People's Money—and How the Bankers Use It* (New York: Stokes, 1914).

16. Ferdinand Pecora, *Wall Street Under Oath: The Story of Our Modern Money Changers* (New York: Simon and Schuster, 1939).

17. Derivatives are financial products constructed or derived from other forms of equity (stocks, bonds, currencies or commodities). Derivatives may be traded on the stock market or outside of it (on the OTC, over-the-counter derivative market). A derivative, mathematically speaking, is the second derivation of the function that expresses the price of a bond with respect to its profitability.

18. Paul Krugman, "Don't Cry for Me, America," *The New York Times*, Op-Ed, January 18, 2008.

19. Joseph Stigliz, "A Bank Bailout that Works," *The Nation*, March 23, 2009.

20. Desmond Lachman, "Welcome to America, the World's Scariest Emerging Market," *The Washington Post*, March 29, 2009.

21. Ronald Dore, "Financialization of the Global Economy," *Industrial and Corporate Change* 17, no. 6 (2008): 1097–1112, originally prepared for the Italian magazine *Stato e mercato*.

Chapter Five: The New World in a Changed World

1. The Fund has finally begun to acknowledge its past policy mistakes with regard to emerging markets and developing economies. In retrospect the Fund's economists now doubt that they knew how to conduct macroeconomic policy, especially their long-held view that unfettered capital flows were fundamentally benign.

2. James Rickards, "How Markets Attacked the Greek Piñata," *Financial Times*, February 11, 2010.

3. See Robert Tornabell, *El dia después de la crisis* (Madrid: Ariel, 2010).

4. The United States is now borrowing record amounts of money, week in and week out, to underwrite a Latin American-like, old- fashioned profligacy. For example, in the week of Thanksgiving 2009 alone, the US was forced to sell $118 billion in debt. That included $44 billion in two-year Treasury notes, $42 billion in five-year notes, and $32 billion in seven-year notes — all record amounts for any single auction.

5. Richard Bernstein, "Chimerica: A Marriage on the Rocks?" *The New York Times*, Letter from America, November 4, 2009.

6. For a clear narrative account by a Wall Street journalist, see David Wessel, *In Fed We Trust: Ben Bernanke's War on the Great Panic; How the Federal Reserve Became the Fourth Branch of Government* (New York: Crown Business, 2009).

7. "Chimericas"—a play on Niall Ferguson's "Chimerica"—is a term of my own invention to denote the incipient close ties between China and Latin America.

8. As reported by Keith Bradsher, "Recession Elsewhere, but It's Booming in China," *The New York Times*, December 10, 2009).

9. The high savings rate in China is largely due to the absence of a national social safety net for health care and old age.

10. There is a reasonable basis for this argument, which President Obama articulated in his Nobel Prize speech in Oslo on December 9, 2009.

11. Felix G. Rohatyn made this argument in *Bold Endeavors: How Our Government Built America, and Why It Must Rebuild Now* (New York: Simon & Schuster, 2009).

12. Cited by Vartan Gregorian, "A Letter from Vartan Gregorian; Literacy Plus Math and Science: An Equation For American Progress," *Carnegie Reporter* 5, no.3 (2009): 41.

13. Horace Mann (1796–1859) was an ardent American abolitionist, social reformer, and visionary educator. One of his outstanding contributions was the transformation of Massachusetts's charity schools for the poor into a great system of free public schools. His arguments in favor of a "common school"—that is, a school commonly supported, commonly attended by all people regardless of race, class or sex, and commonly controlled—was a radical idea that President Domingo F. Sarmiento of Argentina put in practice to great success in the 1870s.

14. To underline the seriousness of this predicament, many US education leaders gathered on June 10, 2009 at the Newseum in Washington, DC to launch a national mobilization to achieve higher levels of math and science learning with the release of the report *The Opportunity Equation: Transforming Mathematics and Science Education for Citizenship and the Global Economy*, The Carnegie Corporation of New York and Institute for Advanced Study Commission on Mathematics and Science Education (2009).

15. Thorstein Veblen, *Imperial Germany and the Industrial Revolution* (New York: Macmillan, 1915).

16. Mancur Olson, *The Rise and Decline of Nations: Economic Growth, Stagflation, and Social Rigidities* (New Haven: Yale University Press, 1982).

17. The Gini coefficient is a measure of income distribution, in which "zero" means perfect equality and "one" complete inequality. The official Brazilian figure is now 0.53 and falling, while China's is 0.47 and rising. (The US figure is 0.41 and India's 0.31.)

18. As reported by Alexei Barrionuevo, "Strong Economy Propels Brazil to World Stage," *The New York Times*, July 31, 2008.

19. With the exception of Chile, this was not the case of other Latin American authoritarian regimes in the 1970s and 1980s.

20. Security in Rio has become an international concern since the International Olympic Committee announced in October 2009 that the city of Rio de Janeiro would be the

site for the 2016 Olympic Games. Brazil is also the site for the 2014 World Cup, which will feature matches in several cities, including São Paulo and Rio.

21. See Jean-Paul Fitoussi, "Following the Collapse of Communism, Is There Still a Middle Way?" in *Political Economy of Modern Capitalism: Mapping Convergence and Diversity*, eds. Colin Crouch and Wolfgang Streeck (London: Sage, 1997).

22. On violent crime and the social cost of inequality, see the excellent Brazilian film *Tropa de Elite* (2007), directed by José Padilha, with Wagner Moura, Caio Junqueira, and André Ramiro.

23. As reported by the world press, Chinese leaders are trying to retool the country's growth model. Previously, they looked to the millions of poor workers—from the country's interior as the engine of a roaring export economy—who would move to coastal provinces, toil in factories, and churn out the world's household goods. These days, the workers are crucial for China's economy in another way: They must start buying the very products they manufacture, spending their paychecks on lipstick and lingerie, plastic lawn chairs, and plasma television sets. Officials see them as the linchpin of China's move away from a lopsided economic model that relies too heavily on foreign consumption.

24. Carlos Garramón, "China: the Strategic Partner for Recovery in Latin America's Southern Cone," *Opinión Sur* 75 (November 2009). Online: http://opinionsur.org.ar/China-the-strategic-partner-for?var_recherche=Garramon (accessed January 2010).

25. Ibid.

26. A *maquiladora* or *maquila* is a factory that imports materials and equipment on a duty-free and tariff-free basis for assembly or manufacturing and then re-exports the assembled product, usually back to the originating country.

27. The *Merriam-Webster Dictionary* defines "chimerical" as a scheme "existing only as the product of unchecked imagination: fantastically visionary or improbable." Online: http://www.merriam-webster.com/.

Chapter Six: Other Capitalisms

1. The recent shift in development thinking—away from the neoliberal presumption that "one size fits all" is reflected in the report of the Commission on Growth and Development, a star-studded group charged by the World Bank with the analysis of "what works" in development. The Spence report (informally named for the commission's chair Michael Spence) represents a watershed for development policy. Gone are confident assertions about the virtues of liberalization, deregulation, privatization, and free markets. Also gone are the cookie-cutter policy recommendations unaffected by contextual differences. Instead, the report adopts an approach that recognizes the limits of what we know, emphasizes pragmatism and gradualism, and encourages governments to be experimental. Successful economies have many things in common: they all engage in the global economy, maintain macroeconomic stability, stimulate saving and investment, provide market-oriented incentives, and are reasonably well governed. It is useful to keep an eye on these commonalities because they frame the conduct of appropriate economic policies. Saying that context matters, does not mean that anything goes. But there is no universal rulebook—different countries achieve these ends differently. The Spence report reflects a broader intellectual shift within the development profession, a shift that encompasses not just growth strategies but also health, education, and other social policies.

The Growth Report: Strategies for Sustained Growth and Inclusive Development, Commission on Growth and Development (Washington, DC: The International Bank for Reconstruction and Development/The World Bank, 2008). Online: http://www.growthcommission. org/index.php?Itemid=169&id=96&option=com_content&task=view/.

2. Eric Hobsbawm, "Socialism Has Failed. Now Capitalism is Bankrupt. So What Comes Next?" *The Guardian*, April 10, 2009.

3. See for example Søren Kaj Andersen and Mikkel Mailand, "The Role of the Collective Bargaining System," in *The Danish Flexicurity Model*, report of the Employment Relations Research Centre, Department of Sociology, University of Copenhagen (September 2005). Online: http://faos.sociology.ku.dk/default2.asp?lan=en&active_page_id=152/.

4. See Timothy B. Smith, *France in Crisis: Welfare, Inequality, and Globalization since 1980* (New York and Cambridge: Cambridge University Press, 2004).

5. It is estimated that in 2010 public debt in Italy will climb to 116 per cent of GDP, four times greater than the limit set by the European Union. Tax evasion grows worse and worse, employment levels are low and pensions absorb 30 per cent of all public spending. Considering that both Italy and Finland form part of the same European Union, the EU seems a bit like a stove with several burners but only one control. For this simple reason, the future of the euro is problematic, and it will not be capable of replacing the dollar as a reserve currency.

6. Per K. Madsen, from the University of Copenhagen, Department of Political Science, has written a synthesis about flexicurity and the Danish model. See Per Kongshøj Madsen, *The Danish Model of "Flexicurity"—A Paradise with some Snakes*, European Foundation for the Improvement of Living and Working Conditions, Brussels, May 16, 2002. Online: http://eurofound.europa.eu/ewco/employment/documents/madsen.pdf/.

Chapter Seven: Rethinking Latin American Dependency

1. Emma Graham-Harrison, "China Splashes Billions on Argentine Rail, Subway," Reuters Africa, July 14, 2010. Online: http://af.reuters.com/article/energyOilNews/idAFTOE66D02J20100714/.

2. Juan E. Corradi, *The Fitful Republic: Economy, Society and Politics in Argentina* (Boulder and London: Westview Press, 1985).

3. See for example, Paul Krugman, "A Model of Balance of Payments Crisis," *Journal of Money, Credit, and Banking* (Ohio State University Press) 11, no. 3 (August 1979): 311–332; and Maurice Obstfeld, "Rational and Self Fulfilling Balance of Payments Crises," *American Economic Review* 76, no. 1 (March 1986): 72–81.

4. See Vincent Ferraro, "Dependency Theory: An Introduction," Working Paper, Mount Holyoke College (July 1996). Online: http://www.mtholyoke.edu/acad/intrel/depend.htm/. One of the best analyses of dependency is one of the very first, and deserves recognition. It was written by the French sociologist Alain Touraine, *Les sociétés dépendantes: essais sur l'Amérique latine* (Paris: Duculot, 1976).

5. Theotonio Dos Santos, "The Structure of Dependence," *The American Economic Review* 60 (May 1970): 231–236.

6. In the standard sociological view, structures are rules and resources (sets of transformation relations) organized as properties of social systems.

7. André Gunder Frank, "The Development of Underdevelopment," *Monthly Review* (1966; repr., June 1989). Online: http://findarticles.com/p/articles/mi_m1132/is_n2_v41/ai_7659725/.

8. Ferraro, "Dependency Theory: An Introduction."

9. Fernando Henrique Cardoso and Enzo Faletto, *Dependency and Development in Latin America*, translated by Marjory Mattingly Urquidi (Berkeley, CA: University of California Press, 1979).

10. Karl Marx, *The Eighteenth Brumaire of Louis Bonaparte*, translated by Daniel de Leon (Chicago: Charles H. Kerr, 1907).

11. See Wolfgang J. Mommsen, *Max Weber and German Politics 1890–1920*, translated by Michael S. Steinberg (Chicago: University of Chicago Press, 1984).

12. Michael Coppedge, "Explaining Democratic Deterioration in Venezuela Through Nested Inference," in *The Third Wave of Democratization in Latin America: Advances and Setbacks*, eds. Frances Hagopian and Scott P. Mainwaring, 289–316 (New York: Cambridge University Press, 2005); also Fernando Coronil, *The Magical State: Nature, Money, and Modernity in Venezuela* (Chicago: University of Chicago Press, 1997).

13. Francisco Rodríguez, "An Empty Revolution: The Unfulfilled Promises of Hugo Chávez," *Foreign Affairs* 87, no. 2 (March/April 2008): 49–62; also Elías Pino Iturrieta, "La Revolución de San Simón," *Letras Libres*, July 2005.

14. This periodization is taken from the research paper by Davide Bradanini, "The Four Americas," Seminar on Political Systems and Institutional Change (Lucca, Italy: IMT, 2009).

15. For a panorama of management in Venezuela, see John Paul Rathborne, "Venezuela Cannot Run on Rhetoric," *Financial Times*, August 2, 2010.

16. Good trend analyses can be found in *China's Expansion into the Western Hemisphere: Implications for Latin America and the United States*, eds. Riordan Roett and Guadalupe Paz (Washington, DC: Brookings Institution, 2008).

17. Kevin P. Gallagher and Roberto Porzecanski, "Climbing Up the Technology Ladder? High-Technology Exports in China and Latin America," *Paper No. 20*, Center for Latin American Studies, University of California, Berkeley (January 2008); Gordon Hanson and Raymond Robertson, "China and the Recent Evolution of Latin America's Manufacturing Exports," in *China's and India's Challenge to Latin America: Opportunity or Threat?* eds. Daniel Lederman, Marcelo Olarreaga, and Guillermo E. Perry (Washington, DC: World Bank, 2009); Rhys Jenkins, "Measuring the Competitive Threat from China for Other Southern Exporters," *World Economy* 31, no. 10 (2008): 1351–1366; Rhys Jenkins, Enrique Dussel Peters, and Mauricio Mesquita Moreira, "The Impact of China on Latin America and the Caribbean," *World Development* 36, no. 2 (2008): 235–253; Luisa Palacios, "Latin America as China's Energy Supplier," in *China's Expansion*, eds. Roett and Paz, 170–189.

Chapter Eight: Latin America in the World of Late Capitalism

1. William I. Robinson, *Latin America and Global Capitalism: A Critical Globalization Perspective* (Baltimore: Johns Hopkins University Press, 2008).

2. In this overview of the domain of globalization studies, I take inspiration from the work of Pierre Bourdieu, especially his analyses of position-takings in the fields of cultural production.

3. Eric Hobsbawm, "Socialism Has Failed. Now Capitalism is Bankrupt. So What Comes Next?" *The Guardian*, April 10, 2009.

4. According to Bourdieu, a field is a setting in which agents and their social positions are located. The position of each particular agent in the field is a result of interaction

between the specific rules of the field, agent's habitus and agent's capital (social, economic and cultural).

5. The concept of risk society was developed by German sociologist Ulrich Beck as part of as theory of late modernity.

6. See Manuel Antonio Garretón et al., *Latin America in the 21ˢᵗ Century: Toward a New Sociopolitical Matrix* (Miami: University of Miami, North South Center, 2003).

7. See Javier Santiso, *Latin America's Political Economy of the Possible: Beyond Good Revolutionaries and Free Marketeers* (Cambridge, MA: MIT Press, 2006).

8. The relative decline in demand for skilled labor may be due to the rise in Latin America of sectors, such as commodities and mining, which are not big job creators. Meanwhile those areas that are generating jobs, such as retail and personal services, require fewer skills. If that is the case, the market may be reducing inequality but also limiting growth.

9. Notably Jorge G. Castañeda, "Latin America's Left Turn," *Foreign Affairs* 85, no. 3 (May-June 2006): 28–43.

Chapter Nine: A Garden of Forking Paths

1. Joyce Appleby, *The Relentless Revolution: A History of Capitalism* (New York: Norton, 2010).

2. On this recasting of "human nature," see the classic article by E. P. Thompson, "Time, Work-Discipline and Industrial Capitalism," *Past & Present* 38, no. 1 (1967): 56–97.

3. Barrington Moore, Jr. discussed the cycle in *Social Origins of Dictatorship and Democracy: Lord and Peasant in the Making of the Modern World* (1966; repr., Boston: Beacon Press, 1993).

4. Emanuel Ionut Crudu, "Exploring the Future of Cuba. Scenarios about the Remains of an Alternative Modernity," Seminar on Political Systems and Institutional Change (Lucca, Italy: IMT, 2009).

5. Albert O. Hirschman, *Exit, Voice and Loyalty: Responses to Decline in Firms, Organizations, and States* (Cambridge: Harvard University Press, 1970).

6. Claudia Hilb, *¡Silencio, Cuba! La izquierda democrática frente al régimen de la Revolución Cubana* (Buenos Aires: Edhasa, 2010).

7. Barrington Moore, Jr., *Terror and Progress, USSR: Some Sources of Change and Stability in the Soviet Dictatorship* (Cambridge: Harvard University Press, 1954).

8. Victor Zaslavsky, *The Neo-Stalinist State: Class, Ethnicity, and Consensus in Soviet Society* (Armonk, NY: Sharpe, 1982).

9. In German, *Das Leben der Anderen*, a 2006 film written and directed by Florian Henckel von Donnersmarck.

10. Juan E. Corradi et al., eds., *Fear at the Edge. State Terror and Resistance* (Berkeley: California University Press, 1992).

11. In part, the "sovietization" of Cuba was a consequence of the spectacular failure of an economically irrational decision by the *Líder máximo*—the failed "record" sugar harvest of 1970, reminiscent of Mao's "Great Leap Forward."

12. Consider the powerful theoretical argument by Charles Tilly, *Durable Inequality* (Berkeley: University of California Press, 1998). For the dysfunctional legacies of Cuban socialism, see Edward Gonzalez and Kevin F. McCarthy, *Cuba After Castro: Legacies, Challenges, and Impediments* (Santa Monica, CA: RAND Corporation, 2004).

13. For an illustration, see another German film, *Good Bye Lenin!* directed by Wolfgang Becker, 2003.

14. For an interpretation that positively values the nature and persistence of a Cuban alternative modernity, see Antonio Carmona Báez, *State Resistance to Globalization in Cuba* (London: Pluto Press, 2004).

15. A useful contribution to this comparison is Benjamin B. Smith, "Life of the Party: The Origins of Regime Breakdown and Persistence under Single-Party Rule," *World Politics* 57, no. 3 (Spring 2005): 421–451. See also Mark P. Sullivan, "Cuba After Fidel Castro: Issues for US Policy," *Congressional Research Service Reports* (Washington, DC, CRS, Library of Congress, 2005).

16. See Joel S. Hellman, "Winners Take All: The Politics of Partial Reform in Postcommunist Transitions," *World Politics* 50, no. 2 (January 1998): 203–34. For a comprehensive review of post-Fidel scenarios, I recommend the research report produced under my guidance by the Romanian doctoral candidate, Crudu, "Exploring the Future of Cuba."

17. An unholy alliance with Venezuela, trading secret-service security for oil, could prop up the Cuban regime in its present shape. The risk of this alliance is that in the end it may accelerate the collapse of both regimes.

18. I heard this comparison made by Roberto Mangabeira Unger, then Minister of Strategic Affairs of Brazil, in a presentation to the Americas Society, New York, April 13, 2009.

19. The term denotes a contraction not only of material dispositions but also of expectations and sociability, as formulated by Philip E. Slater, "On Social Regression," *American Sociological Review* 28, no. 3 (June 1963): 339–364.

20. In 2007–10 (during the world economic crisis) more than 23 million people have risen from lower income classes into Class C, defined as households with monthly incomes between 726 and 1,195 reais ($450 and $745), and which now makes up 46 per cent of Brazil's population. The number of people in the lowest D and E classes fell to 39 per cent of the population in 2007 from 51 per cent in 2005. The figures are from consumer credit firm Cetelem, Itau Bank, and the Central Bank. It is probably one of the biggest social changes since the end of slavery in the nineteenth century. Lower inflation, welfare support, and the level of growth of the economy as a whole have driven these trends.

21. Andrés Malamud, "Liderança sem seguidores: O controverso status do Brasil como potência" ["Leadership Without Followers: The Contested Case for Brazilian Power Status"] (paper presented at the XXVIII International Congress of the Latin American Studies Association, Rio de Janeiro, June 11–14, 2009).

22. For this cursory overview I have relied on the analyses of my doctoral students at IMT, the Institute for Advanced Studies in Lucca, notably Claudia Mancini, "Brazilian Foreign Policy: An Analysis of Current Trends and Future Perspectives;" Valeria Galanti, "UNASUR and ALBA: New Actors in a Multipolar World;" and Pavel Belchev, "The Regional Integration of Latin America," Seminar on Latin American Transitions (Lucca, Italy: IMT, 2009).

23. See Hernando de Soto, *The Mystery of Capital: Why Capitalism Triumphs in the West and Fails Everywhere Else* (New York: Basic Books, 2000); and Roberto Mangabeira Unger, *Free Trade Reimagined: The World Division of Labor and the Method of Economics* (Princeton: Princeton University Press, 2007).

24. The model is in Robert D. Putnam et al., *Making Democracy Work: Civic Traditions in Modern Italy* (Princeton: Princeton University Press, 1992).

25. Felix J. Weil, *Argentine Riddle* (New York: John Day, 1944); Guillermo A. O'Donnell, *Modernization and Bureaucratic-Authoritarianism: Studies in South American Politics* (Berkeley,

CA: Institute of International Studies, University of California, 1972); and Juan E. Corradi, *The Fitful Republic: Economy, Society and Politics in Argentina* (Boulder and London: Westview Press, 1985).

26. On the origins of this perverse pattern, see Carlos H. Waisman, *Reversal of Development in Argentina: Postwar Counterrevolutionary Policies and Their Political Consequences* (Princeton: Princeton University Press, 1987).

27. German for "Night and Fog." It was an instrument of terror and directive of Adolf Hitler on December 7, 1941, resulting in the kidnapping and forced disappearance of many political activists and resistance "helpers" throughout Nazi Germany's occupied territories, principally in Western Europe. For the Latin American version of this method, see Corradi et al, eds, *Fear at the Edge*.

28. An agreement of all political parties on basic policies during the Spanish transition to democracy in 1977.

29. Ipsos Mora y Araujo, *Situación y Perspectivas* 39 (January 2010).

30. Samuel P. Huntington, *Who are We? The Challenges to America's National Identity* (New York: Simon and Schuster, 2004).

31. Kevin P. Gallagher and Timothy Wise, "NAFTA's Unhappy Anniversary," *The Guardian*, January 7, 2010.

32. Jorge G. Castañeda and Héctor Aguilar Camín, "Un futuro para México," *Nexos* (November 2009). Online: http://www.nexos.com.mx/?P=leerarticulo&Article=29024/.

Chapter Ten: The Challenge of Inclusion

1. Tommaso Padoa-Schioppa, *La veduta corta: Conversazione con Beda Romano sul grande crollo della finanza* (Bologna: Il Mulino, 2009).

2. Jacques Attali, *La crise et après?* (Paris: Fayard, 2008).

3. Paul Volcker, "How to Reform Our Financial System," *The New York Times*, Op-Ed, January 31, 2010.

4. Martin Wolf, "The World Economy Has No Easy Way Out of the Mire," *Financial Times*, February 23, 2010.

5. It is a possible scenario foreseen by Jacques Attali in *Tous ruines dans dix ans? Dette publique: la dernière chance* (Paris: Fayard, 2010).

6. Roberto S. Mizrahi, *Adjusting the Course. Getting out of the crisis towards a sustainable development* (Buenos Aires: Editorial Opinión Sur, 2010).

7. Ibid.

INDEX

CPSIA information can be obtained at www.ICGtesting.com
Printed in the USA
BVOW07s1417120614

356208BV00001B/25/P